THE HOLY TEMPLE REVISITED

THE
HOLY
TEMPLE
REVISITED

Rabbi Leibel Reznick

JASON ARONSON INC.
Northvale, New Jersey
London

First Softcover Edition—1993

Copyright © 1990 by Leibel Reznick

10 9 8 7 6 5 4 3 2 1

Original line drawings by David Wilkes.

Library of Congress Cataloging-in-Publication Data

Reznick, Leibel.
    The Holy Temple revisited / Leibel Reznick.
        p.   cm.
    Includes bibliographical references.
    ISBN 0-87668-843-1 (hb)
    ISBN 1-56821-067-1 (pb)
    1. Temple of Jerusalem (Jerusalem)   2. Temple Mount (Jerusalem)
I. Title.
DS109.3.R39   1990
956.94′4—dc20   89-27465
                                                            CIP

Manufactured in the United States of America.
Jason Aronson Inc. offers books and cassettes.
For information and catalog write to Jason Aronson, Inc.,
230 Livingston Street, Northvale, New Jersey 07647.

To Rabbi Berl Wein,
with much appreciation and gratitude.

CONTENTS

ACKNOWLEDGMENT

I would like to thank David Wilkes for his fine line drawings. He endeavored to make them historically and archeologically accurate and they are an invaluable addition to the text. I would like to thank Pinchus Rubinson for the many hours he spent reading and editing the text and for his many suggestions. I would like to thank Eli Mayerfeld for his computer generated diagrams. I would like to thank Ethan Ellenberg, who worked endlessly to see that the book would see the light of day. I would like to thank Arthur Kurzweil and the staff of Jason Aronson for making a dream a reality. Most of all I would like to thank Rabbi Berl Wein, Dean of Shaarei Torah of Rockland County, and my many students, who have enabled, shared, and encouraged my interest in this subject. Much gratitude and appreciation to all of you.

INTRODUCTION

The Holy Temple was the very heart and soul of the Jewish people. Before the First Temple was ever built, King David longed for it. In anticipation, he dedicated his royal treasures to the Temple building. He composed Psalms, liturgical works to be sung in the Temple service.

After the Second Temple was destroyed, Jews yearned to rebuild it. It is now almost 2,000 years since the destruction of the Temple and still, three times each day, Jews express in prayers their hopes for the rebuilding of their Temple. The Temple is not only a proud memory of the past, but represents the future of the Jewish nation.

The future Temple, according to the prophetic visions, will herald an era when no nation will raise up a sword against another, when war will not be taught, and when instruments of battle will be beaten into plowshares. The Jewish Temple is the hope of mankind. The future Temple will be God's palace on earth. God shall reign as King and His subjects will be at peace with one another.

Before the First Temple was built by King Solomon, the son of David, the center of religious activity was in the Tabernacle. This portable sanctuary was like the Jews themselves, a nation of wanderers and conquerors, seeking to possess their promised land. The Holy Ark led them through the desert and accompanied them in battle.

When the Jewish nation became firmly established, it was

necessary to establish a permanent home for God's Sanctuary. God chose Mount Moriah in Jerusalem. Moriah was not an impressive mountain. There were several higher and more majestic peaks nearby. But just as Mount Sinai was chosen because of its modest stature, so, too, Moriah was chosen. This was the traditional site of Abraham's willingness to offer his son Isaac to God. It was where Jacob dreamed of a ladder that reached unto the heavens, a ladder with angels ascending and descending. Moriah represented the humble dedication and dreams of Israel.

The First Temple lasted 410 years. Following its destruction by the Babylonians were the seventy years of exile. At the end of the period of exile, Ezra and Zerubavel built the Second Temple, which endured for 420 years. The Second Temple was destroyed by the Romans in 70 C.E. The institution of the Jewish Temple spanned 900 years.

The twelve tribes of the Jewish nation were divided into three religious classes. The descendants of Aaron, a branch of the tribe of Levi, were the priestly class, the cohanim. They were given the task of performing the sacrifical Temple service. The remainder of the tribe of Levi were the Levites, who performed the Temple's choral and orchestral services. The priests and Levites also served as the elite Temple guards. All members of the priestly and Levite clans belonged to one of twenty-four groups called "mishmoros" or "watches." On a rotating basis, each watch was called to perform the Temple service for one week at a time.

The other eleven tribes were called Israelites. They too were divided into twenty-four groups, called "ma'mados" or "posts." Religious leaders were assigned weeks in which they ceased work and assembled in the synagogues to recite special prayers four times daily and fast during the day from Monday through Thursday. Their prayers were for the welfare and health of the nation. The Temple service was not some far removed holy ritual; all Jews were invited and expected to participate.

Three times each year every Jew was expected to make a pilgrimage to the Temple. During the festivals of Passover, Shevuos, and Succos, Jews congregated in Jerusalem and the heads of the household offered holiday sacrifices. The Temple was included in their joyous holidays.

In addition to the three pilgrimages, farmers brought their first fruits to the Temple as a gift to the Temple priests. The blessings of the field were directly attributed to the beneficence of God and to the priestly Temple service. Israel was divided into geographical districts and the farmers of each district were given an appointed time, between Shevuos and Succos, when they all marched to Jerusalem and paraded through the streets with great pomp. The residents of the Holy City would cease their labors and come into the streets to greet the farmers bearing the priestly gifts.

The land of Israel was divided into twelve states, one state designated for each tribe. Jerusalem was not included in the division. The Holy City belonged to all the people. Just as the people were divided into three classes, the priests, the Levites, and the Israelites, so, too, Jerusalem was divided into three parts or camps. The inner Temple courtyard was the Camp of the Divine Presence, Machne Shechinah. Entry was permitted only to those who were participating in the Temple service. The outer Temple courtyard was the Camp of the Levites. Only those who were not defiled by impurity could enter. The city of Jerusalem was called the Camp of the Israelites.

Sacrifices were divided into three classes. Sacrifices of the first class were completely burned. No part was eaten. Sacrifices of the second class could be eaten, but only by male priests. This sacrificial meat had to be consumed within the confines of the Camp of the Divine Presence. Sacrifices of the third class could be eaten by the family and friends of the person who pledged the sacrifice. These sacrifices could be eaten in the Camp of the Israelites, within the walls of Jerusalem. However, if the sacrificial meat was taken outside the walls of the city, the meat was forbidden to be consumed. The city of Jerusalem was considered an extension of the Temple compound.

Each camp had its own leader. The chief of the Camp of the Divine Presence was the High Priest. He was the supreme authority over the cohanim. The Camp of the Levites was the seat of the Grand Sanhedrin, the Supreme Court, the judicial branch of the Jewish people. The Court was located in the outer Temple courtyard and consisted of seventy-one judges. The Chief Justice was called the Nasi or Prince, and the political and military leader was the Melech, King. His palace was in the Camp of the Israelites, in Jerusalem proper.

In theory, the supreme authority rested with the Grand Sanhedrin and the Nasi. They decided matters pertaining to the Temple rites and declarations of war. The Sanhedrin enacted social and civil law. They were the final arbiters of interpretation of Torah law. The Nasi was considered the king of religious matters; thus, only descendants of King David were elected by the court as Nasis.

However, during the Second Temple Era, there was much conflict between the Nasi and the political king.

To the Jews of ancient Israel, their Temple was the seat of religious rites and judicial authority. Every twenty-four weeks all Jews were invited to participate actively in the service. The Temple was a very real part of their religious, legal, and social life.

One might assume that the Temple only played a role in the life of religious Jews, that to the nonreligious its significance was less important. This was not the case. To all Jews the Temple was highly revered. Jews and their Temple were inseparable. Nonreligious people did not denigrate the Temple rites or the Supreme Court; rather they sought to use their influence to control these institutions, like rival siblings vying for the attention of the parent. Every Jew felt that without the Temple life would be incomplete.

A few years before the Common Era, Herod, King of Judea, rebuilt the Second Temple. It was a most magnificent structure. The rabbis said that it was impossible to conceive of a beautiful edifice without having seen Herod's Temple. Many non-Jews came from abroad to gaze at this architectural wonder and holy site. Many, including Roman emperors, pledged sacrificial offerings.

The Temple was not only the national, judicial, social, and religious symbol of the Jews, it also represented a philosophical concept. It had great kabbalistic meaning. The Temple was the personification of the perfect man. The main sanctuary had two rooms. The upper room was the Holy of Holies and contained the Holy Ark and the tablets with the Ten Commandments. From this room emanated Divine Wisdom, which corresponds to the human mind. The only wisdom the mind of man should endeavor to contemplate is Divine Wisdom, Torah. All other thought is imperfect, false.

The outer room represented the face of man. In the outer room to the upper left was the menorah, and to the upper right was the golden table with the showbread, which correspond to the two eyes of man. The eyes are to be used for two purposes. One is for intellectual pursuits, for enlightenment, symbolized by the light of the menorah. Just as the menorah's fuel was pure oil, so too should man strive for the purity of enlightenment.

The second purpose of man's eyes is for survival: to see and avoid pitfalls, to search out food in order to live—symbolized by the showbread. The showbread was not prepared every day, but rather baked on the Sabbath Eve, left on the golden table for one week, and replaced the following week. The old showbread was divided among the priests on the Holy Sabbath, and although each priest received only a small portion, it was enough to satisfy his desire for food. The perfect man should not pursue food for his own pleasure and indulge in hedonistic practices. Man should eat small amounts of food and only for a higher and holy motive, to endure so that he may serve man and his Creator.

In the center of the room was the golden altar upon which the perfumed incense was offered. This corresponds to the nose in the center of the face. The incense was compounded from herbs and spices that had great mystical meaning. It represented the spreading of pleasantness among men. The offering of the incense was an atonement for gossip and talebearing. Man should strive to make the world a better and more pleasant abode for God's Presence and His creations.

The opening of the sanctuary was located at the bottom of the outer room. It represents the mouth. Here the priests stood when they uttered the priestly benediction every morning. God created the universe with words. His very utterance brought about the various creations. "And God *said*, 'Let there be light!'" Man too has the power to create with his words. He can negotiate peace or declare war. The lesson of the door of the Sanctuary is to use our words to create and to bestow blessings upon our fellow man.

Outside the Sanctuary, in the center of the courtyard, was the altar upon which sacrifices were offered and consumed. This represents the stomach and internal organs of man. Some sacrifices were offered as an atonement for a sin that was committed. Others were offered as a joyous thanksgiving offering. As a general rule, the more grievous the sin, the less was eaten. The more joyous the occasion, the more was eaten and shared. The lesson for man is that the more he merits by performing the mitzvas, the more he will have to enjoy and share.

Man by his very nature yearns to be better. He wants the world to be a better place for himself and his children. Man by his very nature desires knowledge because he is curious about God's creation. Man by his very nature has the desire to love. Love is the feeling of oneness. The ultimate oneness, the ultimate unity, the ultimate love is between man and his Creator. One who strives for all these ideals strives to be the Ideal Man, the Temple-Man.

As long as the Temple stood, man's ideals and goals were obtainable. When the Temple was destroyed, the Temple-Man was destroyed. For two thousand years the Jewish people have prayed for the return of the Temple-Man so that mankind's hopes and ambitions can be realized and fulfilled.

In order to fully appreciate the wonder and glory that once stood in Jerusalem on the Temple Mount, this text has been prepared. It delves into the physical structure of the Second Herodian Temple and reveals the archeological remains that still exist, giving us a glimpse into the past. I have used over 100 different sources, including archeological texts, histories of the period, and rabbinical texts spanning over 2,000 years. Naturally, much of the subject is open for interpretation, speculation, and opinion. Wherever this is the case, I have endeavored to present the conflicting opinions. I have not refrained from stating my own opinions and presenting the evidence.

It is my hope that the readers' interest and intellect will be stirred, so they too may share in the sense of wonder, the feeling of loss, and in the hope of days to come.

THE HOLY TEMPLE REVISITED

Plate 1. The Wailing Wall. One of the first photographs taken of the Western Wall (1865).

1

The Wall

The Western Wall. The Wailing Wall. Wall of stone. Holy stones. Sacred stones. What sorrows they have seen. What secrets they contain. The Wall (Plate 1) watched over our forefathers as they passed this way into the Holy Temple. The Wall watched over our ancestors as they passed this way, driven into exile. The Wall watched as the Romans passed this way to tear down its mighty stones. The Wall watched as the Byzantines passed this way to plow up the sacred mountain. The Wall watched as the Persians, the Omayyads, the Abbassids, the Crusaders, the Mamelukes, the Ottomans, the French, the British, and the Jordanians passed this way to destroy and conquer. But today you still stand watching as we once again pass this way. Your feet are buried beneath the rubbish and debris. Rubbish thrown in hate. Debris thrown with abandonment. Remnants of civilizations long gone. But it is the debris of the Jewish people that lies at the very bottom, and it is the Jewish people who stand on top, embracing your stones, kissing the tears you have held all these years of exile. Into your crevices you receive our bits of paper with our longings and hopes written upon them. Hold them dearly and watch over us, and soon we shall pass by again, into the Holy Temple. May it speedily be rebuilt in our days.

2

The Temple:
A Brief History

The Western Wall is but a small part of a large and majestic enclosure that surrounds a mountain called Temple Mount (Plate 2). It was within this very place that the First and Second Temples of the Jews stood. The wall we see today is a remnant of the Temple wall built by the Judean king, Herod, 2,000 years ago.

The First Temple was built by King Solomon and stood for 410 years. It was destroyed by the Babylonian king, Nebuchadnezzar, in 422 B.C.E., and the Jewish people were exiled from their land. After seventy years of exile, the Persian king, Darius, granted the Jews permission to return and rebuild their Temple. Under the leadership of Ezra and Zerubavel, the Second Temple was constructed. Two hundred years later, the Syrian–Greek Empire, under the rule of Antiochus IV, invaded Jerusalem and captured the Temple. The Temple was defiled with pagan idols and impure sacrifices. Under the leadership of the priestly Maccabean family, the city was recaptured and the Temple was regained. The festival of Chanukah was instituted to commemorate the victory and the miracle of the menorah, which burned for eight days during the Temple dedication service. The Maccabees assumed not only the High Priesthood, but the Judean throne as well. This dynasty, which unified the political and religious houses of Israel, was called the House of the Hasmoneans.

One hundred years later, the Hasmonean rule came to a tragic end. Herod, with the blessings of Rome, became king. The

Plate 2. The Temple Mount. The Dome of the Rock is the focal point of today's site. The upper slope of the Mount of Olives is in the background.

Herodian dynasty lasted about 100 years. In the year 70 C.E., under the rule of Agrippa II, the Second Temple was destroyed by the Roman emperor Vespasian and his son, Titus Flavius.

King Herod built the Temple wall that remains today. How it came to be that Herod built the wall is recorded in the Talmud.

3

King Herod
and Baba ben Butah

Herod (Plate 3) was a slave in the house of the Hasmonean kings. He had his eyes set upon a certain princess. One day he heard a heavenly voice proclaim, "Every slave who rebels will succeed." And so he rose up and killed all the members of his master's house except for the princess he loved. When she saw that he wanted to marry her, she went up to the palace roof and cried out, "Whoever comes and says, 'I am a Hasmonean,' is a slave. For I alone remain from the Hasmoneans and I am throwing myself down from this roof." Herod preserved her body in honey—some say in order to satisfy his desires; others say in order to claim that she survived and he had married a king's daughter.

Herod realized that the rabbis would not recognize his kingship, for the Torah says, "From among thy *brothers* thou shall set a king over you" (Deuteronomy 17:15)—Herod was a slave descended from Edomite converts and was not a blood brother. So Herod rose up and killed the rabbis, sparing Baba ben Butah so he could be counseled by him. Herod placed a laurel of thorns on Baba ben Butah's head and put out his eyes.

One day Herod, disguising his voice, came before Baba ben Butah and said, "See what the wicked slave has done?" "And what would you have me do?" Baba ben Butah replied. "Curse him," said Herod. Baba ben Butah answered, "I am afraid." "But there is no one here but the two of us," said Herod. Still Baba ben Butah would not curse the evil king. Herod then said, "I am Herod, and

Plate 3. King Herod. This statue, found in Egypt, is believed to be of King Herod. It is the only known representation of the Judean king who rebuilt and enlarged the Second Temple.

had I known that the rabbis were so careful, I would not have killed them. Tell me what amends I can make." Baba ben Butah told Herod that the Holy Temple had fallen into a state of disrepair and he should restore it to its proper glory. Herod responded that he was afraid of the government of Rome. Baba ben Butah suggested that Herod send an envoy to Rome to seek permission. The journey to Rome would take one year, the envoy would stay in Rome one year, and the journey home would take one year. Meanwhile, the Temple could be rebuilt.

Which is what Herod did. The Romans sent back a message saying, "If you have not as yet rebuilt the Temple, do not do so. If you have already done so, then you are a bad servant who first does and then asks permission" (Baba Basra 3b–4a).

Herod announced to the people his grandiose plans for the complete rebuilding of the Holy Temple. It would require that the old structure be torn down entirely and built anew. The Jews greatly mistrusted Herod, fearing that he would tear down the Temple and not rebuilt it. Herod therefore promised the people that he would not remove a single stone before all the new materials were prepared and brought to the mountain site (Josephus, *Antiquities,* Book 15, chap. 11, para. 2).

The king paid all the expenses from his own wealth. Horses,

donkeys, oxen, and other beasts of burden were procured. Ten thousand carpenters and craftsmen were hired. Ninety thousand woodcutters and 30,000 stonecutters were employed. Fifty thousand Jews were hired in Jerusalem, and 1,500 priests and Levites were brought to the Temple grounds for the rebuilding. In total, 181, 500 men, Jews and non-Jews, worked on the rebuilding of the Temple (*Yosiphon*, chap. 55).

Herod became king in 37 B.C.E. and began his monumental project of rebuilding the Holy Temple in 19 B.C.E. (Seder HaDoros). (However, according to Sefer HaYuchsin, Herod became king in 23 B.C.E. and began rebuilding the Temple in 8 B.C.E.)

The innermost sacred areas of the Temple took one and a half years to construct. On the day it was completed, which was also the anniversary of Herod's coronation, a large feast was held and the king brought 300 oxen as sacrifices. The remaining outer areas of the Temple took another six and a half years to finish. During that time, it did not rain even once during the day, but rather at night in order that the holy work would not be hindered (Josephus, *Antiquities,* Book 15, chap. 11, para. 6, 7).

4

Herod's Jerusalem

Jerusalem during the reign of Herod (Plate 4) was a marvel to behold. Romanesque architecture and wondrous buildings could be seen everywhere. The Judean capital was truly one of the great marvels of the ancient world. The main gateway to the city was in the middle of the western city wall, about half a mile west of the Western Wall of the Temple. The gateway was protected by three large towers, named for Herod's brother, friend, and wife. The first was called the Phasael Tower, after Herod's brother. It rested on a solid stone base 40 feet long, 40 feet wide, and 66 feet high. Surrounding the top of the base was a wall 16½ feet high. Surrounding the inside of the wall were columns that supported a roof stretching from the top of the columns to the wall. Rising up from the center of the base was a tower reaching a height of 148 feet. The tower was divided into luxurious apartments and baths resembling a prince's palace (Plate 5).

The second tower was the Hippicus Tower, named for Herod's companion, who was killed in battle. The tower rose up 131 feet and contained a large reservoir of water and a garrison (Plate 6).

The third tower was named after Herod's wife, Mariamne. Although this was the smallest tower, rising up only 90 feet, it was the most ornate and luxurious, befitting a tower named after a queen (Josephus, *The Jewish War*) (Plate 7). The gateway where these three ancient towers stood is the site of the present-day Jaffa Gate (Plate 8). Nothing remains of the three towers but the base of

Plate 4. Map of King Herod's Jerusalem.

Plate 5. The Phasael Tower. Artist's impression based on Josephus.

Plate 6. The Hippicus Tower. Artist's impression based on Josephus.

the Phasael Tower, which can be found within the nearby Fortress of David (Plates 9, 10).

To the south of the three towers was Herod's palace (Plate 11). The palace grounds were 1,000 feet long and 200 feet wide and were built atop a 12-foot-high artificially constructed hill. Fifty-foot-high walls surrounded the palace complex. Ornamental towers were mounted on the wall all around. The royal residence was divided into two main sections, one to the north and one to the south. Between them was a park-like mall, with ponds and fountains with bronze figures from which water flowed. There were paths and springs, and tame pigeons hovering about. There were huge banquet halls with high, ornate ceilings and mosaic floors. One hundred guest rooms ornamented with gold and silver objects served to accommodate visiting dignitaries and Herod's entourage.

Today the remains of the palace foundations can be found in the Armenian section of the Old City (Plate 12).

The western district of the ancient city was located atop a hill across from the Temple Mount. It was called the Upper City. In it were the mansions of the wealthy and the estates of the aristocrats. The homes were multistoried and had wooden roofs, a luxury only the wealthy could afford.

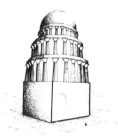

Plate 8. The Jaffa Gate. This is the only western entrance into the Old City of Jerusalem. In ancient Jerusalem as well, the western entrance was located here.

Plate 9. The Fortress, or Tower, of David. Before King David's conquest of Jerusalem, the Jesubites had a fortress on the site. After the capture of the stronghold, David built his fortress and the City of David around this area. For 3,000 years conquering kings have altered and expanded the fortress.

Plate 10. In the present-day Fortress of David stands the base of the Phasael Tower. It was one of the three towers that protected Herod's Palace and the western side of ancient Jerusalem.

Plate 11. The Herodian Palace. Artist's impression based on Josephus.

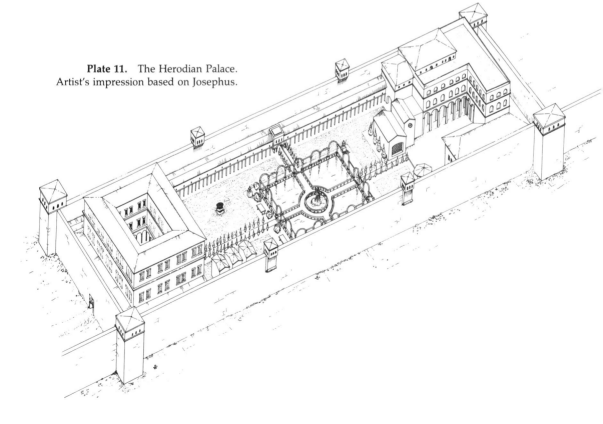

The Upper City hill was actually a mountain, higher than the Temple Mount. On the southeastern slope of the Upper City Hill, facing the Holy Temple, was the Lower City. Here the poorer citizens dwelled. The Lower City's steep streets were no more than a few feet wide. As in all cities, ancient and modern, here misery and poverty dwelled in the shadow of splendor and wealth.

At the eastern base of the hill was the Tyropean Valley, and the street called the Tyropean Way. The derivation of the name is not certain. In Greek, it means "cheesemaker." Perhaps cheese sellers sold their wares in markets in this valley. Perhaps the street was named after a man called Tyropus or Tarphon. The Tyropean Way began in the north of the city at the present-day Damascus Gate (Shar Schechem) and ran southward along the Western Wall of the Temple (Plate 13).

Plate 12. Inside the Fortress of David are the remains of the foundation of the Herodian Palace.

Plate 13. The Damascus Gate. It is also known as the Shechem Gate. During the Second Temple era, the northern entrance of the second city wall was located here. The area outside the wall was the ancient suburbs.

To the south of the Temple was the Ophel. When King David captured Jerusalem from the Jesubites, this was the only section that was inhabited (Plate 14). For most of the First Temple era, this was also the only part of the city in which Jews lived. The Ophel is actually located on the southern slope of the Temple Mount. At the base of the mountain is the Kidron Valley. Along the slope of the mountain is the Ophel, and on top of the mountain, the Holy Temple.

The name Ophel is found several times in the Prophets (2 Kings 5:24; 2 Chronicles 27:3, 33:14; Nehemiah 3:26–27, 11:21; Isaiah 32:14). Many opinions are given as to the derivation of the name. It may mean tower or fortress (Rashi, Chronicles), elevation or rising (Radak, Kings), dark (Metzudos, Kings), or hidden (Targum Yonathan, Kings). The last two references may have to do with the fact that the Ophel was located in the south and had little direct exposure to the sun.

As previously mentioned, during the beginning of the First Temple era the people lived south of the Temple, in the Ophel. Toward the end of that era, the city began to expand southwest onto Mount Zion and eventually north of Mount Zion. This was the Mishna section (2 Kings 22:14; see Rashi). It was probably called the Mishna because the city's second (mishna) wall enclosed this area. During the Second Temple era, the Upper City and Lower City districts were located in the Mishna section. During the final years, the city spread north and northwest of the Temple, into the sparsely inhabited Bethesda, or New City, section.

Plate 14. Ruins in the Ophel—the City of David. The area south of the Temple was the location of the original Jesubite city. During the Second Temple era, this became an exclusive part of the city. A pot was discovered in this ancient home with the name "Achiel" stamped on it.

The original wall around Jerusalem enclosed only the Ophel. When the Mishna section was populated, the wall was extended. This was called the First Wall. It enclosed the south and lower western districts of the old city. The Second Wall was later added to enclose the upper western area. The Third Wall, which was never fully completed, encompassed the north and northwest Bethesda section (see Plate 4).

The Third Wall was constructed of stones 30 feet long, 15 feet wide, and 10 feet high. The height of the wall was 40 feet. Built on top of the wall were ninety towers 325 feet apart. The towers rose 33 feet and contained rooms, cisterns, and great spiral staircases. The Second Wall had fourteen towers, and the First Wall had sixty.

At the northwest corner of the city was the 115-foot-tall Psephinus Tower (Plate 15). It was octagonal, and from its summit on a clear day one could see the Mediterranean Sea in the west and the hills of Arabia in the east.

Plate 15. The Psephinus Tower. This beautiful Herodian tower was located at the northwest corner of ancient Jerusalem. From its summit could be seen the Arabian hills to the east and the Mediterranean Sea in the west.

Plate 17. The stone wall that surrounds Jerusalem today was built in the 1600s by the Ottoman sultan Suleiman. Part of the western city wall was built on top of the remains of the ancient wall that surrounded the Holy City. Note the stones with protruding centers and recessed margins at the bottom of the wall. These date back to the Maccabean era.

Plate 16. The Mount of Olives. Part of this mountain was incorporated into the city limits during the earlier part of the Second Temple era. Today, it is one of the largest and most ancient Jewish burial grounds. Jewish tradition relates that the resurrection of the dead will commence in the valley below. The valley is actually part of the Kidron Valley and is called the Valley of Jehoshaphat. Note the tombs.

Archeologists debate whether the northern third wall was located where the present northern wall of the Old City stands, or if it stood 1,230 feet farther north. Remnants of a wall were found more than 1,200 feet north of the Old City, but it is not known if those are the remains of the Third Wall or of Titus's siege wall around Jerusalem. It is the view of this author that the Third Wall was in fact located over 1,200 feet north of the present-day northern wall of the Old City.

To the east of the Temple Mount is a deep valley called the Kidron, and rising sharply upward to the east of the valley is the Mount of Olives (Har HaZaysim). Throughout the First and Second Temple eras, this area was uninhabited. Today it is the largest and most ancient burial grounds of the Jewish people (Plate 16).

Most of the walls of ancient Jerusalem have been destroyed. The present-day wall surrounding the Old City was built by the Ottoman sultan, Suleiman, in the 1500s. Parts of the Ottoman wall along the east and west of the Old City were built on top of the remains of the old wall. Occasionally, stones from the old wall can be seen. These stones have an engraved margin around the edges and a rough protruding center (Plate 17).

5

The Herodian Stones

The stones used in the great Herodian Temple walls were huge rocks carved into blocks, called ashlars. Most weighed between 2 and 5 tons. However, many weighed 10 tons, some 50, and one in particular weighed almost 400 tons. They were dug out of the quarry by drilling holes in the rock. Wooden pegs were inserted into the holes, and the pegs were soaked with water. As the soaked pegs expanded, the rock cracked, freeing the block from the quarry. The ashlars were carved and finished in the quarry, because metal toolwork was not permitted on the Temple Mount. The finished blocks were hoisted with pulleys, and large wooden wheels were built around the two ends of the block. The block served as a huge axle for the two wooden wheels. Oxen were joined to the wheels and axle, and the ashlars were hauled to the Temple grounds (Plate 18).

Plate 18. Oxen hauling the Herodian stones to the Temple site.

The style chosen for these ashlars was not an original one, but it was unique in ancient Israel and became Herod's trademark. The stones all had a recessed border or margin with a smooth center. The margin was from 3 ½ to 7 inches wide and from ½ to ¾ inches deep. It was not unusual to find, on the same ashlar, margins of different widths and depths (Plate 19).

The stones were hauled into place atop the wall by constructing a large earthen ramp and pulling the stones upward and into place. The wall was three blocks thick at the bottom (16 feet thick) and rose upward about 140 feet. No mortar or cement was used in this Herodian wall. The manufacture of mortar required lime, and lime was made by baking limestone at high temperatures for extended periods of time. This would have required an immense amount of wood for fuel, and wood was a luxury in ancient Jerusalem. The absence of mortar presented a major problem. Usually, when large ashlars were placed one on top of the other, the mortar would soften the impact of descent and prevent the blocks from cracking. Since the Herodian masons used no mortar, pellets of lead were placed on top of the ashlars. When a new ashlar was lowered onto

Plate 19. Typical Herodian Temple stones. When the Judean king, Herod (c. 25 B.C.E.), rebuilt and expanded the Temple, he left his trademark on the stones. They all have recessed margins and smoothly polished centers. The stones of the Wailing Wall are Herodian stones. Over the millennia, rain has worn away the soft limestone. These stones are located on the eastern wall and have been protected by the debris that was piled against it.

a block, the soft lead would ease the impact. The weight of the great stone would then cause the lead to melt and run out from between the blocks (Plate 20).

The mighty walls were three blocks thick. Each row was an-

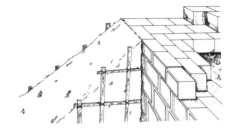

Plate 20. An earthen ramp was constructed so that the huge stones could be rolled into place.

chored to the next with metal braces. In order to stabilize the wall and prevent it from toppling over, the thickness of the wall decreased as it rose upward, giving it a pyramid-like effect.

The wall, because of its tremendous weight, would exert great pressure on the earth below it. To prevent the earth from moving and shifting, causing the wall to collapse, Herod had the wall begin at solid bedrock. Sometimes the bedrock was eighty feet below street level, and it was from here the great wall began its mighty ascent (Plate 21).

Plate 21. The Herodian Temple Wall begins at solid bedrock, about 70 feet below the present ground level.

6

Herod
Extends the Temple

Josephus, in his *Jewish Antiquities*, writes, "And it was in the eighteenth year of Herod's reign that he undertook a very ambitious work, to build the Temple of God, and to make it larger in compass and to raise it to a most magnificent altitude" (*Antiquities*, Book 15, chap. 10, para. 1).

The Holy Temple was built on Mount Moriah. Originally, the Temple walls were not situated at the very base of the mountain but rather part way up the slope. The Temple floor did not rest on the slope of the mountain, but was level with the top of the mountain and extended out over the slope. It was supported by pillars rising from the mountain's slope (Plate 22). This served two purposes. First, because an inclined floor is difficult to walk on, performing the Temple service on a slanted surface would be almost impossible. Second, the rabbis feared that a corpse might be buried beneath the mountain, defiling anyone who walked over the gravesite. The elevated floor would serve as a separation between the worshipper and the burial site (Rambam, chap. 5, Bais HaB'chirah, hal. 1).

Herod's new temple walls were built at the base of the mountain. Herod actually enlarged the Temple Compound. That is what Josephus meant by "larger in compass." When Herod extended the Temple walls to the base of Mount Moriah, he also extended the floor level to reach his new walls. But what would support this floor? He could have built pillars, but they would have had to reach

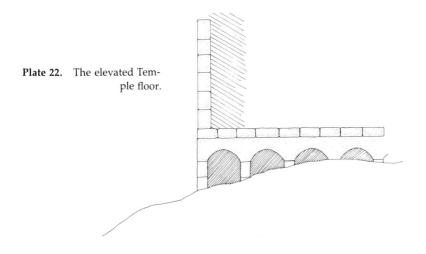

Plate 22. The elevated Temple floor.

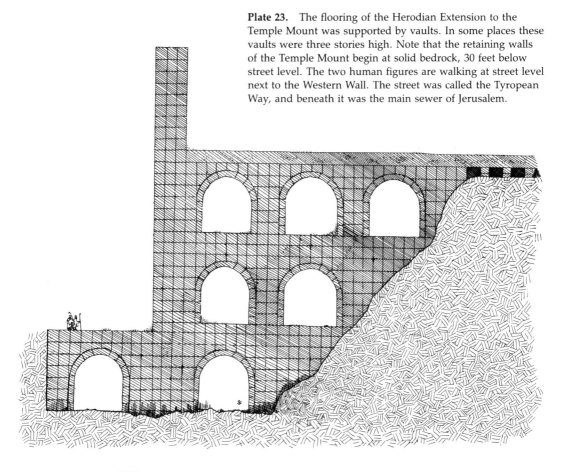

Plate 23. The flooring of the Herodian Extension to the Temple Mount was supported by vaults. In some places these vaults were three stories high. Note that the retaining walls of the Temple Mount begin at solid bedrock, 30 feet below street level. The two human figures are walking at street level next to the Western Wall. The street was called the Tyropean Way, and beneath it was the main sewer of Jerusalem.

much higher than the pillars supporting the original floor. Architecturally this would have been difficult. He could have filled in the void with earth to raise it closer to the floor level, but this would have required a massive earth-moving operation. Instead, Herod built rooms, whole buildings, and vaulted tunnels in the newly created area. He built level upon level, three levels of structures, and resting upon them was the new floor extension (see *Yosiphon*, chap. 55) (Plate 23).

In Jewish law, there is a major difference between the original area encompassed by the Temple walls and Herod's newly added extension. It is well known that anyone who was "unclean" was not permitted into the Temple. The area of the Temple courts could be extended, but in order for the sanctity (kedusha) to be extended also, the extension had to have the approval of the king, the Supreme Court (Sanhedrin), and a prophet, and the High Priest had to consult the priestly breastplate (Urim V'Tumim) (Rambam, chap. 6, Bais HaB'chirah, hal. 11). During the reign of Herod, there was neither a prophet nor the Urim V'Tumim. Therefore, Herod's addition to the Temple Mount would not have any sanctity, and an unclean person would be able to walk there.

Today, since we do not know the exact boundaries and area of Herod's extension, as a rule Orthodox Jews do not walk on any part of the Temple Mount.

Since the Herodian extension had no sanctity (kedusha), it could have been frequented by unclean persons. To prevent them from inadvertently walking into the inner Temple area, the extension was on a slightly lower level and set apart, with a wall separating the two areas. There was probably no direct access from the extension into the main Temple grounds.

The Temple floor was about 100 feet above the street level. To get from the city streets to the top of the Temple Mount, one could either climb monumental staircases or pass through underground tunnels that led to the top of the mountain.

7

Contradictions

The Talmud devotes an entire tractate, Midos, to the Temple structure. Midos was composed by the Sage Rabbi Eliezer ben Yaakov (Yoma 16a), who lived during the time of the Herodian Temple (Seder HaDoros). He describes the structure thus: "The Temple was 500 cubits long and 500 cubits wide" (Midos 4:1). "The Temple had five gateways. On the southern side were the two Chuldah gates. To the west was the Kiphonus gate. In the north was the Tadi gate, and to the east was the Shushan gate" (Midos 1:3).

Rabbi Eliezer ben Yaakov tells us that the Temple wall was 500 cubits on each side and that there was *one* gateway on the western side, called the Kiphonus Gate.

The Jewish historian, Josephus Flavius, author of *Jewish Antiquities,* lived during the time of Rabbi Eliezer ben Yaakov. Josephus recorded for posterity his own description of the Temple walls: "On the western side of the Temple wall there were *four* gates. The first led to the king's palace. Two more led to the suburbs, and the other led to the valley by a great number of steps" (italics added) (Josephus, *Antiquities,* Book 15, chap. 11, para. 5).

Here we have a contradiction between a respected rabbinical scholar and a noted historian. There are those who question the accuracy and authenticity of Josephus's reportage; however, the *Sefer Yosiphon* (chap. 55), which was also composed by Josephus, contains exactly the same quote as the Josephus *Antiquities* text.

Josephus wrote two accounts of Jewish history in general and of the Second Temple era in particular. The first, written in Aramaic, is called *Yosiphon* or *Sefer Yossef ben Gurion HaCohain*. It was later translated into Hebrew. The second work was written in Greek and consisted of two books, *Jewish Antiquities* and *The Jewish War*. They were composed primarily for the European intelligentsia. Some scholars believe that the Greek version contains hyperbole, unreliable historical data, and a condescending Roman bias. However, the reliability of the *Sefer Yosiphon* can hardly be questioned. The giant among biblical commentators, Rashi, quotes from the *Sefer Yosiphon* no fewer than nineteen times. Other respected rabbinic authorities who used the *Yosiphon* text include Rabbaynu Saadyah Gaon, Rabbaynu Gershom, the Baal HaAruch, Rashbam, Baalei Tosfos, Raavad, Baal HaMeor, Ibn Ezra, Ramban, Abarbanel, Maharal M'Prague, Bach, and Tosfos Yom Tov.

Another major problem to be solved is Rabbi Eliezer ben

Plate 24. The Temple Mount. A general view of the Temple complex as seen from the southwestern corner. The "viewer" is standing on the roof of one of the mansions in the Upper City.

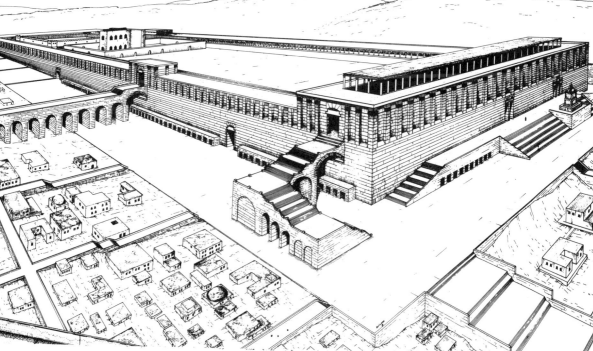

Yaakov's contention that each wall was 500 cubits in length. The Temple walls are visible to this very day. Each wall has a different length. Their lengths are as follows:

Western Wall	1,601 feet
Southern Wall	922 feet
Eastern Wall	1,530 feet
Northern Wall	1,042 feet

It is well known that there is a question among present-day scholars as to the exact length of a cubit (amoh). The opinions range from 18 inches to almost 24 inches. Even if a cubit were 24 inches, 500 cubits would equal 1,000 feet. The Western Wall should therefore be at the most 1,000 feet long. However, in fact, the Western Wall is over 1,600 feet long.

The solution to the problem is that Rabbi Eliezer ben Yaakov is describing the inner sacred areas of the Temple. The areas that Herod added are not included in Rabbi Eliezer ben Yaakov's account, for they have no sanctity. Josephus, on the other hand, is describing the entire Temple Compound, including the Herodian extension. The wall of the inner sacred area was only 500 cubits, and had only one gateway on the western side. That wall no longer stands. However, the outer area, the Herodian extension, was over 1,600 feet long and had four gateways on its western side. That is the wall Josephus describes, and it is that wall that still stands today (Plate 24).

8

The Western Wall

AS IT WAS IN THE TIME OF HEROD

The Western Wall of the Herodian Temple (Plate 25) was 1,601 feet in length. Running alongside was the Tyropean Way. The white flagstone street was 52 feet wide, with 10-foot-wide sidewalks on each side of the street. Stone-walled shops lined the sidewalks. All the stores had front doors and interconnecting doorways between one store and the next, indicating cooperative or corporate ownership, possibly by the Temple treasurers.

The street was paved with large limestone tiles weighing about five tons each. Each tile was 6½ to 12 feet square. Beneath the Tyropean Way was the vaulted main sewer for the city, and running off the main sewer were smaller ones that routed the drainage water from the Upper and Lower City into the main system. The water was carried out to the Kidron Valley at the base of the Ophel.

During times of danger, the sewers of Jerusalem became safe havens. The people would wait in the arched tunnels, unable to stand fully erect, until the danger passed. (The danger did not always pass.)

The Western Temple Wall rose 105 feet above street level. The upper 33 feet of the wall had projecting stones that formed the likeness of columns, called pilasters. The same design can be found on the outer walls of the Cave of the Patriarchs (Ma'aras HaMachpelah) in Hebron, for they, too, were built in the Herodian style, probably by King Herod (Plate 26).

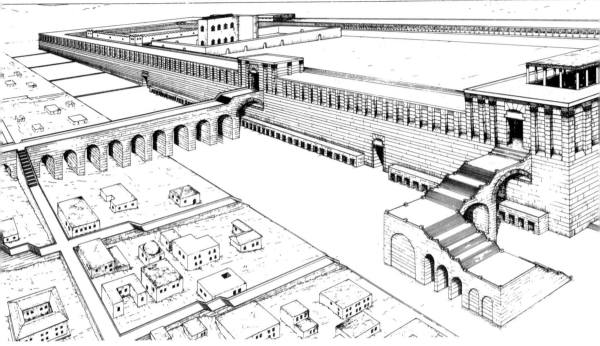

Plate 25. The Western Wall. Along the Western Temple Wall were four entrances into the Holy Temple. The first was to the right. It was a monumental staircase, supported by a series of arches, leading into the southern section of the mountain. The second entrance was a gateway that led into an underground tunnel that surfaced on the top of the mountain. The third was a bridge supported by a series of arches that led to the western section of the Mount. The fourth entrance was the Kiphonus Gateway that led underground and surfaced inside the sacred area of the Temple.

Toward the southern end of the Western Wall was the great southern archway (Plate 27). It began 39 feet from the southern end of the wall. The span began at the Temple floor above, crossed 42 feet over the Tyropean Way, and came down to the base of the Lower City. This southern arch rose 80 feet from the ground, and was 50 feet wide. Very likely, it was the largest arch constructed to date.

Near the great arch were six consecutively smaller arches going southward toward the Ophel. Steps led from the street up to the top of the first arch, and other steps led from the top of the first arch to the top of the higher second arch. From the top of the second arch, more steps led to the top of the even higher third arch, until eventually the top of the great arch was reached. On top

Plate 26. The wall at the Cave of the Patriarchs, Ma'aras HaMachpelah. The wall probably was built by King Herod and was fashioned after the Temple Wall.

Plate 27. The Southern Archway. The steps led up from the Tyropean Way to the Royal Basilica in the southern part of the Temple Mount. This was the highest underpass ever built up to that time.

The Western Wall in Herod's Time **27**

of the Great Southern Arch was a landing that led into the southern section of the Herodian extension to the Temple. Built into the base of all these arches were interconnecting stores.

Extending from the middle of the Western Wall was another series of arches going westward toward the Upper City. This series formed a bridge supporting a roadway that led from the western Herodian extension to the king's palace (Plate 28).

Between the southern arch and the king's archway was a large gateway 18⅓ feet wide and 36⅔ feet high. This doorway and its dimensions were typical of all the Temple doorways, its height being double its width. The lintelstone was 25 feet long, 7 feet high, and weighed 50 tons.

This middle gateway led under the Temple Mount. The passageway had a large domed ceiling and ran eastward for about 70 feet. The passageway then turned toward the south, slowly inclining upward for 55 feet. It led up to the southern Herodian extension.

Toward the northern end of the Western Wall was another gateway, whose dimensions were the same as those of the middle gateway. Near the outside of the gateway was a wonderful garden with all types of roses. This was the only garden permitted in Jerusalem, for its rose petals were used in the compounding of the Temple incense (Baba Metzia 72b, see Rashi). The gateway was called the Kiphonus Gate. Kiphonus means "rose garden" in Greek (Shiltai HaGiborim). Some say the name is a corruption of the Hebrew phrase "klapai naice" (opposite the miracle). The Holy of Holies was a chamber of miracles, and this doorway was not only the closest to the Holy of Holies, but led directly toward it (Raavad). Others say that Kiphonus in Greek means "greatest," for this gateway was the closest of all the outer gateways to the Holy of Holies (Rosh). Some say the gate was named after an official called Kiphonus, who donated the funds for it (Tiferes Yisroel, Midos 1:3). The Kiphonus gateway led straight under the Temple Mount. Unlike the middle gateway, it turned neither left nor right, but rather led upward until it finally reached the Temple floor, about 150 feet in back of the Holy of Holies. This is the only western entrance that led from the Tyropean Way into the inner sacred precincts of the Temple. The other gateway and two archways led only to the Herodian extension, and there was no access from the extension courtyard into the inner Temple area.

Outside the Kiphonus Gate, to the right, built into the wall, was a most unusual stone, a single ashlar 42½ feet long, 13 feet high, 10 feet thick, and weighing 400 tons. It is the largest single building

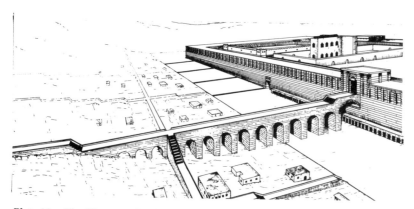

Plate 28. The Kingsway Bridge. This bridge led from the Herodian Palace into the Temple.

stone in the world, and dwarfs the other Herodian stones. Why such a large stone was placed there is a mystery.

The Herodian wall, which rises 105 feet from the street level, actually begins below street level at solid bedrock. At the southern end of the Western Wall, bedrock is about forty feet below street level. Toward the northern end of the Western Wall, bedrock is at street level, and at the very northern end of the wall, the bedrock reaches above the street level. In fact, the back wall of the stores that were located at the northern end of the Western Wall was the bedrock itself.

9

The Western Wall

AS IT IS TODAY

The Western Wall that we stand before today is but a small segment of the original Herodian Western Wall. Half the wall lies buried seventy feet beneath the ground. The upper portion of the wall, which consists of smaller blocks cemented together, are from much later Arab periods. The entire northern half of the Western Wall is almost completely hidden by the Arab houses in the Muslim quarter of the Old City.

Of the two Herodian gateways and two arches, only small hints are left, mere traces and shadows of the past. Of the southern arch, only a few stones projecting from the wall remain. These stones are called springing stones, because from this point the arch sprang forth from the wall (Plate 29). It is called Robinson's Arch, after the American historian Edward Robinson, who discovered it in 1838. The base of the pier of the arch, where it came down on the other side of the Tyropean Way, has been unearthed in recent years. It, too, consisted of the Herodian bordered stone. The remains of four shops that were built into the pier have also been discovered (Plate 30).

The king's archway, extending from the middle of the wall, was torn down during the destruction of the Second Temple. In later years the Muslims rebuilt it with new stones, as the old stones were buried under debris. This Muslim reconstruction can be seen inside the tunnel, directly to the left of the Western Wall (Plate 31). It looks like a vaulted tunnel and is called Wilson's Arch, named

Plate 29. Robinson's Arch. This is the remnant of a monumental arch-supported stairway that led from the street to the top of the Temple Mount. In the text it is referred to as the southern arch.

Plate 30. The remains of the southern arch's pier (Robinson's Arch). Stores were built into the pier. Shopkeepers catered to the needs of the pilgrims who constantly poured into the city.

Plate 31. Some people think that the arch located near the left of the Wall is Wilson's Arch. Actually, Wilson's Arch is located inside that tunnel (see Plate 32).

after the British archeologist and surveyor Charles Wilson, who discovered it in 1865. The original springing stones can still be seen projecting from the wall (Plate 32). Modern-day archeologists, digging seventy feet below the arch, have found the original stones that formed the Herodian king's archway.

Several areas of the old Tyropean Way street have also been unearthed, and beneath it the original Herodian sewers (Plates 33, 34). In Herodian times, across the Tyropean Way were two public buildings. One was called the Xystos, whose function is not known for certain. Perhaps it was a public assembly hall. The other building was the Counsel, where all official documents were stored. During the final years of the Second Temple, the Zealots tried to encourage the people to arm themselves and fight the Romans. They were opposed by the rabbinical authorities, who urged a peaceful settlement with the enemy. The Zealots burned down the Counsel building, destroying all documents, including letters of indebtedness, hoping that those who benefited would join the Zealot ranks.

In the nineteenth century, the remains of a public building were discovered forty feet below the area in front of the Western Wall. It

Plate 32. Wilson's Arch is the remnant of a series of arches that supported a bridge that led from the Judean king's palace directly into the Temple. Today, Jews can be found at all hours of the day and night under the archway, praying for the coming of the Messiah and the rebuilding of the Holy Temple.

Plate 33. The street level of ancient Jerusalem was located 30 feet below the level of the present-day Western Wall Plaza. In Temple times it was called the Tyropean Way. Some of the original flagstones of the street were unearthed south of the Western Wall.

had arched ceilings and was lined with stone columns. Since no indication of fire or soot was found, in all likelihood it is the remains of the Xystos rather than the Counsel. The Xystos was built during the Hasmonean era, before Herod, and therefore lacks the usual Herodian stones. Josephus refers to the Xystos six times, using it as a focal point of ancient Jerusalem.

Only a fraction of the lintelstone of the middle gateway, which stood between the king's archway (Wilson's Arch) and the southern arch (Robinson's Arch), can be seen today. In the women's section of the Wailing Wall, there is a stone room built against the wall, which the women use for prayers when it is raining. That room blocks most of the lintelstone, but a small portion is still visible. In contrast to most Herodian stones, which are about 3½ feet high, this lintelstone is 7 feet high and can be discerned by looking for the stone that is twice as high as the others (Plate 35). The lintelstone and its gateway are called Barclay's Gate. They were named after their discoverer, J. J. Barclay, an American diplomat sent to Jerusalem in 1856 to repair the Dome of the Rock.

The Western Wall Today **33**

The passageway that led from the middle gate under the mount and turned southward toward the southern Herodian extension is still there. Centuries ago the Muslims converted it into an underground mosque and called it El Buraq. It has long since fallen into disrepair and disuse, and has not been explored since the mid-1800s. In medieval times the entranceway was blocked with smaller stones.

There are no photographs or drawings of this passageway (Plate 36), but Charles Wilson, who visited the passageway in April 1866, describes it as follows: "The passageway runs east, with an apparently level floor, for a distance of 69 feet, where it enters some sort of vestibule with a domed roof. In the north wall of the vestibule is an arched recess. In the center of the dome is a circular opening to admit light. Then turning south, it appears to reach to surface by an incline. The floor is covered by more than 20 feet of rubbish. This section is 40 feet wide and 54 feet long. Everything has suffered much from hard usage and the walls are thickly covered with cement, hiding the character of the masonry" (*Ordnance Survey of Jerusalem 1866*, p. 89).

Plate 34. The remains of the sewer that ran under the Tyropean Way. This sewer was in use for almost 2,000 years, until 1967.

Plate 35. To the right of the large growth cluster is a large stone. It was the lintelstone of a gateway that led into a tunnel that ran under the Temple Mount and surfaced at the top. The lintelstone was about 27 feet long, most of it hidden by the building adjacent to the wall. Under the lintelstone can be seen the small stones that block up the doorway. Two-thirds of the height of the gateway lies buried under the ground. This Temple tunnel was used by the Muslims as a mosque, called El Buraq, and was never fully explored.

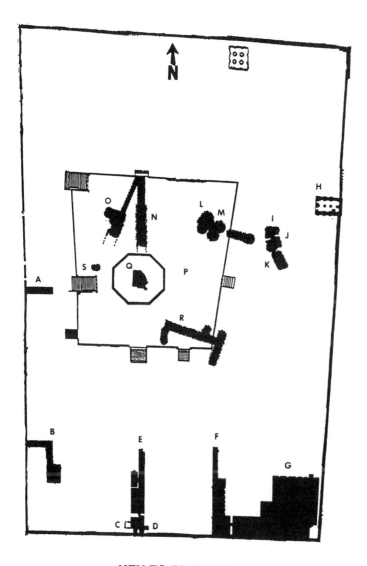

KEY TO PLATE 36

A– WARREN'S TUNNEL
B– BARCLAY'S TUNNEL
C– TOMB OF SONS OF AARON
D– ROOM OF ELIJAH
E– CHULDAH TUNNEL EXIT
F– CHULDAH TUNNEL ENTRANCE
G– KING SOLOMON'S STABLES
H– MERCY GATE
I– CISTERN #14
J– CISTERN #13

K– CISTERN #12
L– CISTERN #2
M– CISTERN #34
N– CISTERN #1
O– CISTERN #3
P– DOME OF THE ROCK PLATFORM
Q– THE ROCK
R– CISTERN #5
S– CISTERN #4

Plate 36. Archeological map of the Temple Mount.

Of the Kiphonus Gate that led under the Herodian extension to the sacred Temple precincts, nothing is left to be seen from the outside of the wall. Arab houses block it from view. During the Middle Ages, the Crusaders altered the Kiphonus Gate by giving it an arched top. The arch can be seen 131 feet north of Wilson's Arch, and is evidence of the ancient Kiphonus Gate. It is called Warren's Gate, named after a member of Wilson's surveying team. The rest of the Kiphonus Gate is still buried. In recent years a small synagogue has been constructed in front of the Kiphonus Gate, and it is the closest Orthodox Jews can get to the site of the Holy of Holies (Plate 37).

Plate 37.   Warren's Gate. The remains of the ancient Kiphonus Gate. This section of the Western Wall has not yet been opened to the general public. A small synagogue has been built in front of the sealed gate and is used on special occasions. The Kiphonus Gate led into a 50-foot-long tunnel that surfaced in the sacred Temple precincts. This tunnel has never been explored, either.

The passageway that led from the Kiphonus Gate (Warren's Gate) under the Herodian extension to the floor of the Temple is still there. It was used as a cistern by the Muslims for many centuries. It is now filled with debris and filth and has never been explored (see Plate 36).

Since the entire upper portion of the Herodian wall has been knocked down, the pilasters (projecting stones forming a column) cannot be seen. In one Arab house built against the Western Wall, a section of the upper wall remains, together with a fragment of a pilaster. The pilastered wall built by Herod in Hebron, which surrounds the Cave of the Patriarchs (Ma'aras HaMachpelah), still stands. Not only do these walls give striking solemnity and dignity to the burial site of our ancestors, but they also hint at the beauty that once surrounded our holy Temple.

10

The Southern Wall

AS IT WAS IN THE TIME OF HEROD

The Southern Wall, like the Western Wall, was built by King Herod. It was 922 feet long, and had two large gateways, 230 feet apart, called the Chuldah Gateways (Midos 1:3) (Plate 38). The prophetess Chuldah sat near here during the final years of the First Temple, admonishing Jewish women to give up their idolatrous ways. When the Second Temple was built, these gateways were named after Chuldah (Tosfos Yom Tov), for it was here that she sat and near here that she was buried. Although burial in the city of Jerusalem itself was not permitted, exceptions were made for the Davidic kings and for Chuldah (Baba Metzia 72b).

These doorways were the main entrance and exit of the Temple: The gate to the right served as the entrance, and the gate to the left the exit. Both led into long tunnels extending under the southern Herodian extension up into the upper sacred area. Passing through these tunnels made one feel like a weasel ("chuldah" in Hebrew), which is why some say they are called the Chuldah Tunnels (Rosh).

The tunnels are 295 feet long and 42 feet wide. Just inside each gateway is a large room with beautifully decorated domed ceilings supported by large columns and arches. The entrance gateway room had nine domes, three rows with three domes in each row. The exit gateway room had four domes, two rows of two domes each. These rooms were about 65 feet long and 42 feet wide. Beyond these anterooms were the tunnels. The tunnels themselves

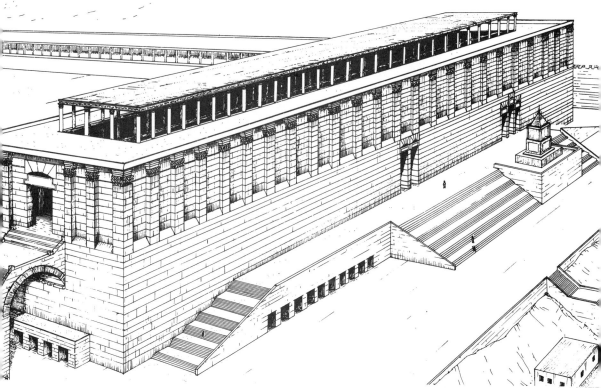

Plate 38. The Southern Temple Wall. The triple gateway was the main Temple entrance and the double gateway was the main exit. The monument between them was the tomb of the prophetess Chuldah who prophesied here during the final years of the First Temple. The southern gateways were called the Chuldah Gates. Above the Southern Wall is the largest Temple Building, the Royal Basilica.

were 203 feet in length and had vaulted ceilings. The tunnels were built on an upward incline so that the upper end of each tunnel was 28 feet higher than the lower end. At the ends of the tunnels were flights of steps bringing the worshipers upward another twenty feet, so that they stood in the southern section of the sacred area of the Holy Temple.

In the anteroom of the entrance gate, to the right, was a door leading into a maze of vaulted tunnels and chambers. This complex was used for storage and was over 35,000 square feet. (An average room in a home is about 156 square feet; therefore, this complex was the size of 225 rooms.) There were two more levels of underground structures beneath this level. Those levels were not

The Southern Wall in Herod's Time **39**

Plate 39. The Tomb of Helena, a non-Jewish queen who converted to Judaism during the Second Temple era. She lived her final years in Jerusalem and had a palatial residence south of the Temple, in the Ophel.

used, and it is said that they were secret exits from the Temple above.

Passing along the base of the Southern Wall was the Southern Walkway, which was twenty feet higher than the Tyropean Way. At the southwestern corner of the wall, a flight of steps brought the worshipers up from the Tyropean Way to the Southern Walkway. At the other end of the walkway was another flight of steps leading downward. The Southern Walkway was 918 feet long and 23 feet wide for most of its width. Between the two Chuldah Gates, the walkway was much wider, forming a public square.

From this public square worshipers had a marvelous view of the city. In front, the Southern Wall of the Temple rose majestically. Behind them was the Ophel, sloping steeply downward to the Kidron Valley. In the Ophel they could see the synagogues and houses of learning and the palatial Complex of Queen Helena, the queen of Adiabene who converted to Judaism. Adiabene was a country on the banks of the Tigris River (Plate 39). To the west worshipers could see the Lower City slowly rising from the Tyropean Way. Majestically crowning the top of the Lower City hill was the Upper City and its mansions and palaces. The three

Herodian towers could be clearly seen. To the east was a spectacular view of the southern side of the Mount of Olives and the olive orchards with their thickly gnarled trunks.

The entire walkway was supported by the roofs of interconnecting stores built underneath. In front of the stores was the upper Ophel Way, running parallel to the Southern Wall. It was possible to go directly from the upper Ophel Way to the entrance Chuldah Gate by climbing a flight of thirty steps. These steps were 50 feet wide and 9 to 10 inches high. The depth of the steps alternated between 12 and 36 inches. There were also steps in front of the exit Chuldah Gate. They were very similar to the entrance steps except that they were 215 feet wide. During the festival seasons, tens of thousands of holiday pilgrims hurried up and down these steps with their sacrificial animals. Mikvas could be found everywhere, as one who was unclean could not enter the Temple grounds.

During the busy festival seasons, the stores could hardly keep up with the demand. Most of the storekeepers in the area sold livestock and fowl for sacrifices. Out of necessity many of the pilgrims slept outside the city, because the overcrowded city could not accommodate the great multitude. There were about 100,000 permanent residents of Jerusalem, but when the pilgrimages came, the population swelled to over five million.

11

The Southern Wall

AS IT IS TODAY

Of the entire Herodian Temple Complex, the most significant archeological remains are to be found in the vicinity of the Southern Wall (Plate 40). Today there are six gateways built into the wall. Facing the wall, starting from the right, is a single arched doorway called the Single Gate (Plate 41). Next to it are three

Plate 40. The Southern Temple Wall.

Plate 41. The Single Gate. This gateway was built by the Crusaders as an entrance into the lower level of the Temple, called King Solomon's Stables. This gateway, like all the other Temple gateways, was sealed up by the Muslims.

arched gateways called the Triple Gate (Plate 42). To the left is a double arched gateway called the Double Gate. All were built at least a thousand years after the destruction of the Temple. All have been sealed up with stone walls. A Crusader tower was built next to the Southern Wall; it completely covers the left Double Gate and blocks from view half the right Double Gate (Plate 43). Although no remains of the Chuldah Gates are to be found, there are a few telltale signs that mark their exact location.

The Single Gate was built entirely of smaller stones. Not a single Herodian ashlar was used in its construction. It was built by the Crusaders around the year 1100 and was used as an entrance into the lower Temple complex.

The Triple Gate, however, does contain a Herodian stone at the base of the left doorpost. The question has been posed as to whether this is the location of some Temple Gate or if this gateway, like the Single Gate, is of later construction. When Herod had Temple gateways built, the right and left gateposts had decorative molding carved on the outside. On the Triple Gate, the Herodian stone at the bottom of the far left doorpost still has this decorative molding (Plate 44). This indicates that it is a Temple gate. We can

Plate 42. The Triple Gate. In Temple times a triple gate was located in the southern Temple wall. It was called the Chuldah Gates and was the main entrance into the Temple. It led 300 feet under the Temple Mount and surfaced at the top.

now at least place the left doorpost of one of the Chuldah Gates. But was the Chuldah Gate a large single gate, a double gate, or even a triple gate similar to the one that is there today? This question will be resolved shortly.

The Double Gate contains a sign of the presence of a Temple gate. As mentioned earlier, most of the Double Gate is blocked by the Crusader tower. On the small portion that is exposed are the remains of a Byzantine cornicestone (Plate 45). An important feature of Herodian architecture was to be seen above the lintel-stone. A series of stones, forming a small arch, spanned the lintel (Plate 46). Above the Byzantine cornice, part of this Herodian arch can be seen, indicating another Temple gate (Plate 45).

In the time of the Temple, these doorways led to anterooms, which in turn led to the Chuldah Tunnels; they are still there today. In centuries past, they, too, were used as mosques called El Kadimah. The domes in the anteroom ceilings remain with a small portion of the decorative floral and geometric design still showing (Plates 47, 48). Huge monolithic columns with unusual floral capitals still rise from the floor to support arches holding up the

Plate 44. The stones that flanked the Temple gateways had a wavy pattern, called molding, carved into them. This is one of two such surviving stones. It is located at the bottom of the left arch of the Triple Gate. The other stone is above Robinson's Arch but can only be seen from inside the Temple Mount.

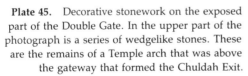

Plate 43. The Double Gate. One and a half gates were blocked by a Crusader addition to the Southern Wall. In Temple times a double gate was located here and served as the main Temple exit.

Plate 45. Decorative stonework on the exposed part of the Double Gate. In the upper part of the photograph is a series of wedgelike stones. These are the remains of a Temple arch that was above the gateway that formed the Chuldah Exit.

Plate 46. Typical Temple gateway. The Temple's gateways had three unique characteristics. The Herodian stones forming the side of the doorway had a molding design carved into them. Above the doorway was a unusually shaped lintelstone. Over the lintelstone was an arch. No Temple gateway remains intact today; however, fragments of each of these characteristics can be found in different places around the Temple Mount (see Plates 35, 44, and 45).

Plate 47. The Chuldah Tunnels had lines of columns supporting large domes. Many fragments of the decorative designwork that adorned these domes have been found. This is an artist's reconstruction of one of the domes.

Plate 48. A fragment from one of the domes. Note the swastika-like design.

great domes. These primitive columns may very well be remains from the First Temple, built by King Solomon (Plates 49, 50, 51).

In the anteroom of the western Chuldah Gate sealed doors lead to small chambers. The chamber to the right of the anteroom is called Elijah's Place by Muslims. The chamber to the left of the anteroom is called the Tomb of the Sons of Aaron (see Plate 36).

The left Chuldah Gate's anteroom has four domes, 16½ feet in diameter. They are in two rows of two domes. The right Chuldah Gate's anteroom has nine domes in three rows of three domes. This indicates that the left Chuldah Gate was in fact a double gate, similar to the one there today, and the right Chuldah Gate was a triple gate, similar to the Triple Gate that stands today.

The great underground complex remains. When the Crusaders captured Jerusalem, they converted this structure into a stable that could accommodate thousands of beasts, and called it King Solomon's Stables (see Plate 36). In truth, it was not King Solomon's, nor was it a stable. It was built by King Herod to support the floor above (Plate 52).

Before the June war of 1967, everything below the southern gates was covered by 2,000 years' accumulation of rubbish and debris. After the Old City was regained and the Temple grounds were once again in Jewish hands, archeologists began the tedious process of exposing whatever was hidden below. The buildings of the Jordanians covered the remains of the Ottoman buildings. The remains of the Ottomans were atop the Muslim ruins, which covered traces of Crusader buildings. The vestiges of the Crusaders were above the Byzantine ruins, which were above the Roman remains, which buried the remnants of the buildings of the Jews. In time, archeologists uncovered parts of the Temple that had not been seen in over 1,000 years.

Plate 49. An accurate depiction of the inside of the Chuldah Tunnels. The capitals of the columns are from a more primitive era, possibly the First Temple.

Plate 50. Inside the Chuldah Entrance Tunnel. In this 80-year-old photograph, the sun above the Temple Mount is shining in from the northern end of the Tunnel.

Plate 51. Inside the Chuldah Exit Tunnel. In this old photograph, we are looking south from inside the Tunnel and can see the Double Gate from this position.

Plate 52. View of the great underground complex built by Herod to support the floors above.

Expanses of the Southern Walkway were rediscovered (Plate 53). The steps upon which our ancestors trod were unearthed (Plate 54). These steps are mentioned in the Talmud (Berochos 58a) and in the Tosephta (Sandehrin 2:2). Several stores were found, covered with ash and soot, evidence of the destruction of the Second Temple (Plate 55).

Below the base of the steps in front of the Double Gate a secret passageway leading under the Temple Mount was found. Its walls had small niches, or recesses, carved into them to hold small oil lamps that provided light in this dark tunnel. The passageway led to a level below the underground Chuldah Tunnel. It was blocked up with earth after sixty-five feet. The remains and artifacts found in the blockage were those of the Jews of the Second Temple era. No evidence of later periods was found, indicating that the Jews were the last to use this tunnel.

A century earlier, Charles Warren had found another tunnel leading under King Solomon's Stables. It was blocked after ninety-eight feet. This tunnel is located 112 feet west of the southeast corner of the wall. It is 3 feet wide and 11½ feet high. The stones inside are Herodian ashlars.

Plate 53. The remains of the walkway that ran along the Southern Temple Wall.

Plate 54. The steps that led up to the Chuldah Gates. Our ancestors trod upon these very steps on their way into the Holy Temple.

Plate 55. The remains of stores that ran along the Southern Wall beneath the walkway. They were destroyed almost 2,000 years ago, about one month after the Roman invaders destroyed the Temple.

Plate 56. An ancient public mikva. This mikva, located several yards in front of the foot of the Southern Wall steps, was used by those seeking entrance into the Temple.

Plate 57. General view of the ruins in front of the Southern Wall.

Plate 58. Around 130 C.E., the Roman emperor Hadrian converted the Holy Temple into a pagan temple. One of the dedication plaques was later rebuilt, upsidedown, into the Southern Wall near the Double Gate.

Some of the steps that led up from the Tyropean Way to the Southern Walkway have also been unearthed. Near the base of the steps, leading from the Upper Ophel to the Southern Walkway, several large public mikvas have been found (Plate 56). A multitude of buildings and homes of Turks, Muslims, Christians, Persians, and Romans have been discovered. But it is the remains of the Jews that are at the bottom, and it is the Jews who today are standing on top, digging down through eras and epochs, through nations and civilizations, through the crumbled legacy of tyrants and emperors who sought to eradicate the Jewish memory from the history of man (Plate 57).

In the year 135 C.E., sixty-five years after the destruction of the Second Temple, the Roman Emperor Hadrian put down the Bar Kokhba rebellion. Hadrian built a pagan temple where the Jewish Temple had stood. Much of the original Temple structure was still standing and was incorporated into the pagan building. The city was renamed Aelia Capitolina, and Jews were forbidden to be seen within sight of the city, under penalty of death. Centuries later, one of the dedication stones honoring Hadrian was rebuilt upside down into the Southern Wall. It is located to the upper right of the Double Gate (Plate 58).

12

The Eastern Wall

The Eastern Temple Wall had one gateway called the Shushan Gate (Midos 1:3). The Persian emperor Darius II, the child of Xerxes (Achashvayrosh) and Esther, gave the Jews permission to rebuild the Second Temple (Rashi, Ezra 1:1). The capital of the Persian Empire was Shushan. As a token of indebtedness, the Jews placed a carving of the city of Shushan above the gateway (Tosfos Yom Tov), some say at the insistence of the emperor (Rav; compare Menachos 98a). Other opinions maintain that an entire structure was built over the Shushan Gate with the carvings of Shushan in or on it (Rashi, Menachos).

Engraved onto the wall outside the Shushan Gate were two markings indicating the length of a cubit. One marking was to the right of the gateway, one to the left. The marking on the wall to the right was half a "finger's width" (etzbah) smaller than a true cubit. The marking on the left wall was a full "finger's width" larger than a true cubit (Kelim 17:9). Workers, who were paid in lengths of wood, were paid according to the smaller marker. Workers hired to cut a certain length of wood would measure it according to the larger marking. Whoever pledged a length of inexpensive material to the Temple would measure it according to the larger marking; whoever pledged a length of expensive material, such as a precious metal, would use the smaller marker (Menachos 98a).

King Solomon built a special two-chambered room in the Temple. One chamber was for bridegrooms and the other for mourners. Those who visited the Temple went to offer the appropriate words either of congratulation or condolence (Sofrim 19:12).

The Eastern Wall of the Temple Compound was 1,530 feet long. The only visible structure is a large building built into the wall with a double-arched gateway, which has been sealed for centuries. It is known as Mercy Gate (Shar HaRachamim). Some call it the Golden Gate (Plate 59). The style of the decorative stonework is Byzantine, similar to the cornicestone above the Double Gate. It is not known whether this gateway is an original Temple building. It is too far off the ground to have been used in Temple times as a gateway. If it was a new building and not a gateway, what was its purpose? Who built it? And why? The Christian Byzantines did not have any particular regard or reverence for the Temple Mount. Why would they build on top of it?

Medieval Jewish travelers and commentators have said that the Mercy Gate is the remains of King Solomon's room for mourners and grooms (Kaftar V'Ferach). Perhaps it is the remains of the structure above the Shushan Gate upon which the Persian capital was engraved.

Another bit of speculation about the origin of the Mercy Gate is based on the procedure regarding the "red heifer." The red heifer was slaughtered and burned on top of the Mount of Olives, directly across from the Shushan Gate. The priest who prepared the animal was supposed to be able to see the gateway of the Heichel, the main Temple building on top of the mountain. Before Herod's time, the Eastern Wall was lower and did not block the priest's view (Midos 2:4). Herod raised the wall; however, in order not to obstruct the view, he left a large opening or window in the wall. When the Byzantines captured the Temple grounds, they filled in this open space with the Mercy Gate. But why such an ornate gateway with a beautiful room was needed is not known. Speculation about this has been going on for centuries.

Access to the inside of this structure can be obtained from inside the Temple Compound. Within are domed ceilings supported by columns. Josephus describes the columns used in the Temple as being of the Corinthian order. This classical Roman style of architecture employed columns whose capitals were very ornate, consisting of three tiers of large acanthus leaves. Some of the columns inside the Mercy Gate are Corinthian (Plate 60).

Tradition says that Elijah will herald the coming of the Messiah by walking through the Shushan Gate. Therefore, the Muslims have built an Arab cemetery along the Eastern Wall to foil Elijah's

Plate 59. The Mercy Gate. Some believe that this ancient structure, built onto the Eastern Temple Wall, is the remains of a First Temple structure built by King Solomon. It was constructed with two rooms, one for bridegrooms and the other for mourners. Temple visitors would enter these rooms to offer the appropriate words of congratulations or condolences.

plan, for Elijah is from the priestly clan, and a priest may not defile himself by entering a burial ground (Plate 61). The Talmud relates that a discussion arose as to whether a priest may enter a non-Jewish cemetery. The opinion of Elijah himself was sought, and he answered that priests may enter a non-Jewish cemetery (Baba Metzia 114b). Obviously, the designer of the cemetery was not a talmudic scholar.

Plate 60.   Inside the Mercy Gate.

Plate 61.   Jewish tradition says that in the Days to Come Elijah and the Messiah will lead the Jews triumphantly into the Holy Temple through the eastern Temple gateway. To thwart their plans, the Muslims have built a cemetery along the Eastern Wall so that Elijah, who is a priest, cannot defile himself by entering these burial grounds.

In all likelihood, the Shushan Gate is still in existence, buried beneath the Arab cemetery. A few years ago, a photographer was taking pictures of the Mercy Gate while standing in the Muslim cemetery. He suddenly lost his footing and fell into a large opening beneath one of the tombstones. He found himself in a cavern filled with bones, and at the end of the cavern was a section of the Eastern Wall below the Mercy Gate. The wall had a sealed archway in it, indicating the site of an ancient gateway, the Shushan Gate (Plate 62). The Mercy Gate today has a double gateway built into it. Both gates are sealed. The remains of the Shushan Gate are located beneath the left sealed arch of the Mercy Gate. In all probability,

Plate 62. Under the Muslim cemetery, in front of the Mercy Gate, is a cavern filled with bones. In the back can be seen the curved stones that formed an arch over the ancient Shushan Gate. Courtesy: James Fleming. Biblical Archeology Review (January/ February 1983).

there is also another gateway to the right, under the right sealed arch of the Mercy Gate. This means that the Shushan Gate was also a double gateway, similar to the double gate of the Chuldah Exit.

A tunnel led from the Shushan Gate up to the sacred areas of the Temple. Nothing is known about this tunnel, but it is probably still there today.

A most interesting phenomenon can be noticed on the Eastern Wall. Herodian style ashlars were described earlier as having a recessed margin with a smoothly polished center. The stones along the Eastern Wall, from the Mercy Gate to 105 feet before the end of the Wall, do have a recessed margin, but the center is rough, unfinished, and protruding (Plate 63). We have already noted that Herod extended the Temple Mount. We know that he made western and southern extensions by moving the Western and

Plate 63. Along the Eastern Wall are stones with rough, protruding centers. These are not Herodian (see Plate 19). Possibly, they are the remains of a First Temple era wall.

Southern Walls outward. Later we will discuss the northern extension. But did Herod also move the Eastern Wall outward?

The stones along the Eastern Wall, with the rough centers, are from an earlier period. Herod could not and did not move the Eastern Wall forward. At the base of the steep slope upon which the Eastern Wall stands is the Valley of Yehoshafat. If Herod had moved the Eastern Wall to the bottom of the valley, the wall would then have had to rise 300 feet to be even with the other walls surrounding the Temple Compound. Therefore, Herod decided not to move the wall.

Since the Southern Wall was moved, the Eastern Wall would have to be extended in order to reach the Southern Wall. When a wall is extended, a vertical line, or seam, is formed. One hundred and five feet from the southern side of the Eastern Wall is a seam (Plate 64). The stones to the south of the seam are all typically Herodian. To the north of the seam, the stones all have rough centers. We can determine now that Herod added 105 feet onto the Temple Mount to form his southern extension.

Whether the section of Eastern Wall with the rough-centered stones is from the First Temple or from an era as late as that of the Hasmoneans cannot be determined with any degree of accuracy.

However, remains of the Phasael Tower (see Plate 10), which was originally built by the Hasmoneans, can be seen to this day. Its stones have margins with rough protruding centers, similar to the ashlars of the Eastern Wall. Careful scrutiny reveals, however, that the centers of the Eastern Wall ashlars protrude much more than those of the stones of the Phasael Tower.

To the left of the seam are the remains of an arch. Its springing stones are Herodian and therefore must date back to the time of the Second Temple. The top of this archway did not lead to the floor level of the Temple, as did Robinson's Arch and Wilson's Arch on the Western Wall. This arch led into King Solomon's Stables, the lower level of the Holy Temple.

In the late nineteenth century, Charles Warren sank a shaft near the southeastern corner of the Temple Wall. His objective was to determine how far down the southeastern corner went before it hit bedrock. To his amazement, the wall went down eighty feet before hitting solid rock. The total height of the wall at that point must have been close to 200 feet. Josephus describes the view from the top of this corner: "Looking down into the valley from these

Plate 64. To the right of center is a vertical line, called a seam. When a wall is extended, a seam is formed. The original Eastern Wall was built with the stones to the right. They have rough, protruding centers. Herod added the segment of wall to the left when he enlarged the Temple Compound. His stones have smoothly polished centers. The protruding stones in the Herodian sector are the remains of an arch that led from the street into King Solomon's Stables.

heights would make one giddy: the bottom of the valley could not be seen" (*Antiquities*).

Warren also made the amazing discovery that the foundation stones contained Phoenician lettering (Plate 65). Some of the letters were carved onto the stones, and some were written in red ink. These letters were marks to identify stones in order to set them into their correct positions. It is known that King Solomon used Phoenician workers in the building of the Temple (1 Kings 5:32); however, these letters were found on Herodian stones. Phoenicia ceased to be a country right before the reign of Herod. There are two possible ways in which Phoenician letters could come to be on post-Phoenician stones. Either Herod employed workers who still used the Phoenician alphabet, or he reused and recarved some of the stones from the Solomonic Temple in his reconstruction of the Second Temple.

Pottery was also discovered by Warren at the base of the southeastern corner. The pottery is Graeco-Phoenician, dating from the end of the Phoenician era, which would date the stones to the Herodian period. It is interesting to note that the columns that Herod built consisted of a series of drums. The drums had to fit exactly, one atop the other, in order to form a perfect column. The stonecarvers would mark the bottoms of the drums to indicate exactly which drum fit where. The bottoms of the drums were marked with Hebrew lettering.

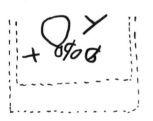

Plate 65. Phoenician lettering found on the bottom layer of stones near the southeastern corner of the Temple Mount.

13

The Northern Wall

There was one gateway in the 1,042-foot-long Northern Wall. It was called the Tadi Gate (Midos 1:3) (sometimes called Tari Gate [Tiferes Yisroel]). All the other Temple gateways had the same basic rectangular shape—only the Tadi Gate was unique. Some say that the sideposts of the doorway leaned inward and met at the top of the doorway (Plate 66). Others picture the doorposts as upright and parallel. However, at the top two upward-reaching lintel-stones leaned against each other, forming the top of a triangle (Plate 67). (According to the Tiferes Yisroel, the word "tari" is related to "tri," from which the word triangle is derived.)

The name Tadi comes from the Greek word meaning "high." The angle formed at the top made this doorway higher, or taller, than the others (Rosh). Others say Tadi is derived from a word meaning "private," since this doorway was not used by the general public, rather by mourners and those placed under a ban for refusing to comply with a court order (Tiferes Yisroel). Some say the name Tadi derives from a word meaning "poems," as the Levites had a room nearby in which they learned psalms, or poems (Tosfos Yom Tov). Still others say Tadi derives from a word meaning "weak" or "leaning," because the two lintelstones were leaning one against the other (Shiltai HaGiborim). Others derive the name from "summer," as during the heat of the summer the Northern Wall offered shade in which the people would sit (Shiltai HaGiborim). Still others say Tadi is a man's name, Teddy—Theodorus (Radak).

64 THE HOLY TEMPLE REVISITED

Plates 66 and 67. Two versions of the Tadi Gate.

Plate 68. Berachas yisroel, the remains of a cistern built by Simon the Just in the third century B.C.E. It was located against the left side of the Northern Temple Wall. In this old photograph (1865) can be seen two ancient tunnels. Where they led was never fully determined. The area was partially filled in during the British Mandate and has been completely covered over in recent years.

Toward the left side of the Northern Wall was a very large cistern called the Israelite Pool (Birachas Yisroel). It was also called Bethesda Pool, because the northern suburb of Bethesda was nearby. It was 360 feet long, 126 feet wide, and 80 feet deep. It was built in 250 B.C.E. by Simon the Just (Shimon HaTzaddik).

No visible signs of the Tadi Gate can be discerned today; however, the site of the Israelite Pool can easily be noticed along the eastern part of the Northern Wall (Plate 68). The northern Temple wall forms the back wall of the cistern. Little archeological work has been done in this area. The pool is filled with garbage and filth. To the west are two parallel vaulted tunnels that run along the Northern Wall westward. These tunnels, like the cistern, are cemented, indicating that they were used to hold or conduct water. These tunnels are also filled with rubbish and have never been fully explored.

(**Note:** In the past year, a public plaza has been built over the site of the Israelite Pool. The pool and the water tunnels can no longer be seen.)

14

The Antonia
and the Royal Basilica

Herod extended the original Temple Mount in three directions, north, south, and west. The northern extension was occupied by a fortress called the Antonia, named after Mark Antony (Plate 69). Originally built at the very beginning of the Second Temple Era, it was later strengthened by the Hasmoneans and called Baris, or Birah. The ceremonial garments of the High Priest were kept there.

Herod completely rebuilt the fortress. It was constructed on a rock 82 feet high, because in the northwestern sector of the Temple compound, the bedrock rises far above the ground level. The sides of this large rock were covered with smooth flagstones, both for ornamentation and to make climbing impossible. Atop the rock was a stone wall 5 feet high surrounding the fortress. The fortress rose 65 feet from within these walls.

The interior resembled a palace, with chambers, halls, and baths of every description. There were great courtyards for the stationed troops. Antonia was like a royal town. In each corner of the fortress were towers 82 feet high. The southeastern tower was 115 feet high. Beneath the southeastern tower was a secret passage for Herod to enter the sacred precincts (*Antiquities*, Book 15, chap. 11, para. 7).

The Antonia Fortress occupied the northern Herodian extension. It extended all the way from the Western Wall to the Eastern Wall.

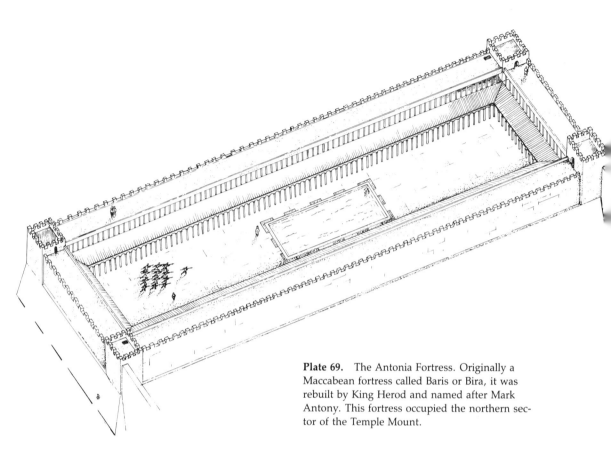

Plate 69. The Antonia Fortress. Originally a
Maccabean fortress called Baris or Bira, it was
rebuilt by King Herod and named after Mark
Antony. This fortress occupied the northern sector of the Temple Mount.

Strategically, the Antonia was the key to the Temple (*Antiquities*,
Book 15, chap. 11, para 4; *The Jewish War*, Book 5, chap. 5, para. 8).

The Talmud gives two opinions regarding the name Birah. One
commentator says that the entire Temple Mount is called Birah. His
view is substantiated by the verse, "Unto Solomon, my son do
Thou give . . . to do all and to build the Birah" (1 Chronicles
29:19). The second view says that Birah refers to a specific portion
of the Mount (Pesachim 104a)—the fortress (Pesachim 7:8).

Archeologists believe that the Antonia Fortress was located
outside the Herodian extension to the northwest. This author does
not share that belief for reasons too numerous and esoteric to
elaborate upon. In either event, there are no known remains of the
Antonia today. Should investigations atop the northern sector of
the Temple Mount ever be allowed, undoubtedly some of its ruins
will be found.

In the southern extension was the largest building on the entire Temple Mount, the Royal Basilica (see Plate 38). Basilica refers to a style of architecture to which this structure conformed. It extended 922 feet from the Western to the Eastern Wall and was 105 feet wide. Four parallel rows of Corinthian columns, with forty columns in each row, went from west to east. The four rows of columns formed three aisles; the two outer aisles were 30 feet wide and 50 feet high, and the center aisle was 45 feet wide and 100 feet high, a single story. The beams and ceilings had deep carvings of all sorts, and the building was fashioned of polished stone.

The Royal Basilica occupied the entire southern extension. Because its width was 105 feet, we can conclude that Herod expanded Har HaBayis southward 105 feet. As we know, the Eastern Wall consisted of pre-Herodian stones up to 105 feet before its southern end. At that point, a vertical line or seam indicated an extension to the wall. That line marks the beginning of the southern extension.

Although this was the largest structure on top of the entire Temple Mount, the purpose and function of the Basilica is not recorded anywhere. The Talmud tells us that when the Sanhedrin (Supreme Court) ceased to judge capital offenses, they moved from the Supreme Court chambers to the "shopping mall" (Rosh HaShana 31a). This shopping mall was located on the Temple Mount (Rashi). The halacha (Jewish law) states that carrying money in an open or public manner is forbidden on the Temple Mount, as the Temple is a place of holy worship and should not appear to be an area of commerce (Tosfos, Pesachim 7a). Now, if merely giving the appearance of commerce is forbidden, how much more so is the actual location of stores and shops atop the Mount. Perhaps this shopping mall was located within the Royal Basilica. Because this area was built on Herod's extension, it did not have the sanctity of the Temple itself, and commerce would have been permitted.

The Talmud says that the Supreme Court chambers were a "basilici" (basilica) (Yoma 25a). It's not clear if the Talmud is describing the original building or if it is referring to the Royal Basilica.

Today, the site of the Royal Basilica is occupied by the El Aksa Mosque (Plate 70). Parts of the interior are patterned after the original Herodian structure.

Herod also extended the western part of the mountain. He did not extend the eastern side; that had already been done in earlier

Plate 70. The El Aksa Mosque. In Temple times the largest Temple structure was located here. It was called the Royal Basilica. In the later Temple era, it served as the seat of the Grand Sanhedrin. Part of the El Aksa is patterned after the original Temple structure.

years, perhaps even during the reign of King Solomon (Josephus, *Antiquities*).

Surrounding the entire extension was a double row of columns made of white polished stone. The columns were 40 feet high and supported a wooden roof of cedar wood. This type of structure is called an arcade or stoa. The width of this arcade was 50 feet. The natural magnificence of its ceiling was so wondrous a spectacle that no carving or ornamentation was required (*The Jewish War*, Book 5,

Plate 71. Surrounding the inside of the Temple walls was an arcade with a wooden roof. During the destruction of the Second Temple it was these roofs that burned. Most of the Temple structure was fashioned out of brick and rock.

chap. 5, para. 2) (Plate 71). Today, a Muslim arcade has replaced the original Temple structure (Plate 72). An old adage in archeology says that walls have a memory. It means that very often a modern wall or building will stand on the site of a much older, similar structure. Here we have a modern arcade on the site of an older one.

Herod constructed four large porticos for the Temple Mount. A portico is a large hall used as an entranceway. Each portico faced in each of the four directions, north, south, east, and west. Each portico was 375 feet long, 150 wide, and 180 feet high. Each had 160 stone columns (*Yosiphon*, chap. 55). It is not clear if the porticos were located in the Herodian extension or if they were on sacred precincts.

Plate 72. In Temple times, an arcade surrounded the inside of the Temple Mount wall. It was later rebuilt by the Muslims.

The Antonia and the Royal Basilica **71**

15

The Temple Mount

The focal point of the Temple Mount was the central courtyard containing the sacred area. Outside the courtyard were many rooms and buildings. The exact location of these various chambers is not known. A partial list of their functions includes:

1. House of Study (Bais Medresh), in which the talmudic law was taught and discussed.

2. Lounge for minor Temple officials.

3. Chamber for Levite guard officials.

4. Weapons room, in case of enemy invasion.

5. Toolroom for repair work.

6. Curtain weaving and storage, also called the Chamber of Elazer (Elazer was a well-known weaver who fashioned the curtains that separated the Holies from the Holy of Holies).

7. Chamber for priest and Levite supervisors, including the waker of the priests, who woke them for the morning service. The priests had sleeping quarters in the Temple courtyard. This chamber also served as the office for the choirmaster of the Levites and the leader of the Levite musicians, who sang and played during the Temple service.

8. Shekel treasury. Every Jew was expected to contribute one half shekel a year toward the cost of the sacrificial animals.

9. Storage for Holy Service utensils.

10. Service utensil donations room.

11. Anonymous charity for the poor. The anonymous giving of charity was the highest level of social righteousness. Donations could be deposited secretly in the room, and the monies were dispensed secretly to the needy.

12. Lulav (palm branch) storage. In the Temple, the palm branch was used every day of the seven-day Succoth Festival, including the Sabbath. Every day the people would bring the palm branches from their homes to the Temple for this service. However, carrying any item in the streets on the Sabbath was prohibited. Therefore, the palms were brought to the Temple and placed in this chamber on Friday for use the next morning.

13. Soiled priestly garment storage, used in the making of wicks for the Temple's candelabra.

14. Trumah and ma'aser tithe storage, for specific priests or Levites. Ancient Israel was primarily an agricultural society. The people were dependent upon the blessings of the land. In accordance with Torah law, at the time of the harvest Jews gave tithes to the priests, the Levites, and the poor to show their appreciation for their blessings. One fiftieth of all produce grown in the Holy Land was given as a trumah tithe to the priests. One tenth of the produce was given to the Levite as a ma'aser tithe. The priestly and Levite tithes were signs of recognition of the fact that it was due to the merit of the Temple service and the adherence to the Torah that the blessing of a rich crop was bestowed upon the nation. The tithe could be given to any priest or Levite in the land; however, many chose to give it to particular priests or Levites who were serving in the Temple.

15. Ma'aser tithe storage, for general consumption of Levites. Any produce brought to this chamber could be taken by any of the Levites serving in the Temple.

16. Trumas ma'aser tithe storage, for general consumption of priests. The Levites had to give one-tenth of the tithes they received as a trumas ma'aser tithe to the priest.

17. Firstborn animal offerings. The firstborn male of a kosher, domesticated animal was brought to the Temple and left as a gift to the priests, who would offer the animals as sacrifices.

18. First fruits offering storage. The first fruits that grew in the Holy Land were brought to the Temple as a gift for the priests. Each geographical district in the Holy Land would choose a week in which the farmers would march in a procession through the streets of Jerusalem and into the Temple. Amid much pomp and ceremony they would present the priests with their gifts.

19. Trumah and challah tithe. Any produce in this room was trumah tithe for any serving priest. Bakers had to give a portion of each batch of dough, or a portion of bread baked from that batch, to the priests as a challah tithe.

20. Chamber for shekel donations.

21. Donations for Temple renovations and repairs.

22. Lumber storage.

23. Infirmary, also called the Chamber of Ben Achiah, a renowned doctor to the priests. Priests were often subject to stomach ailments, due to the large amount of sacrificial meat they had to consume.

24. Chamber for gifts (charamim) for the priests. This was not an obligatory tithe, but rather a gift offered by individuals out of respect and appreciation for the priests and their sacred tasks.

25. Office of the priestly chaplain.

26. Chamber of the lockers of the gates.

27. Amrachlin chamber, used by seven lower treasury officials.

28. Chamber of the Vice High Priest (Segan Cohain Gadol).

29. Katlukin chamber, used by two assistants of the Vice High Priest.

30. Chamber of the officers of the Israelites (ma'amod). All priests, Levites, and Israelites were divided into twenty-four groups. Each week a different group of priests and Levites would serve in the Temple. The Israelites of that group would conduct special synagogue services during their week. Officials would be appointed for each of the three groups. This room was for the officers of the Israelites.

31. Supervisory personnel, also called the Chamber of Matisyah ben Shmuel, a renowned supervisor of the Temple service.

32. Treasurers' office. At least three officers shared this office. Their task was to collect the funds pledged toward Temple upkeep.

33. Synagogue. This building was located on the eastern side of the Temple Mount.

34. Stone house, where the ashes of the red heifer were stored and prepared. All the utensils were made of stone, which were not susceptible to defilement. This building was located to the northwest.

35. Trumpet place. The shofar (ram's horn) was sounded from the roof of this building before the onset of the Sabbath to let the people know when they must refrain from work. A watchtower was built nearby.

(Numbers 1 through 35 are based on Shekalim, chap. 5 [Jerusalem Talmud].)

36. Inside the Eastern Gateway of the Mount, to the north, was a lower judicial court. There were three

lower courts in Jerusalem. One was located in the former Hasmonean Palace, which was to the west of the Western Wall. Two others were located on the Temple Mount. This is one of them (Tiferes Yisroel).

Each of the three lower courts was presided over by twenty-three judges who sat in a semicircle. The head of the court sat in the middle. Before the judges were three rows of benches, occupied by sixty-nine apprentice judges. The last seat was filled by the last apprentice to join the court. The first seat was filled by whoever was there the longest. Whenever a vacancy on the judges' bench occurred, the student who occupied the first seat would be elevated. All the other students then moved up one seat, creating a new last seat vacancy, which would be filled.

No remains of any of those buildings have been found. However, a plaque with the inscription, "l'bais hatokeah l'hac . . ."—"To the Place of the Trumpet of the c . . ."—has been found outside the southwest corner of the Temple Wall (Plate 73). This inscription is somewhat of a puzzle. Since this was not a place of public assembly, why would a plaque indicating its location be necessary? Perhaps it was a dedicatory plaque, "For the Place of the Trumpet, donated by c," with "c" the name of the benefactor or his family.

An earthen vessel with a picture of two birds upside down and the inscription "korbon" (sacrifice) has also been found (Plate 74). Two birds and an earthen vessel were used in the purification procedure of a healed leper (Leviticus 14:5).

Plate 73. A plaque with the engraving *L'Bais Hat'kiya–To the Place of Trumpeting*. This plaque was found southwest of the Temple Mount.

Plate 74. A vessel with the word *Korbon–Sacrifice* carved on it. Also engraved, upsidedown, were two birds.

16

The Cheil

The main section of the Temple Mount was the central courtyard, called the Azarah, based on the phrase, "Send forth Your help (ezrecha) from Your holy place" (Psalm 20:3). The Azarah was rectangular in shape and was surrounded by a high wall.

Surrounding the Azarah was a large square courtyard. It was called Har HaBayis, or Mountain of the House, by the sages. It was 500 cubits square (Midos 2:1) (Plate 75), and surrounded by a very high wall. However, the eastern wall of Har HaBayis was lower than the others, in order not to block the view of the entranceway to the Heichel building (Plate 76) from the priest who was slaughtering the red heifer on the Mount of Olives (Yoma 16a).

Surrounding the central Azarah courtyard, ten cubits away from its wall, was a low wooden fence, called the Soreg (Plate 76, #1). It was ten fists (t'fachim) high (about 36 inches), and consisted of woven wooden slats laid crosswise, similar to room dividers (Midos 2:3; Rav).

According to some authorities, the purpose of this fence was to permit carrying within the Temple compound on the Sabbath. Although the complex was completely surrounded by walls, carrying on the Sabbath within a walled area was usually permitted only if the walled area contained houses or other structures suitable for habitation built *before* the fence or walls were constructed (see Shulchan Orech, Orech Chaim 358). The walls of the Holy Temple were built before the house. Therefore, to permit

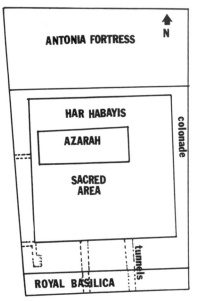

Plate 75. The Temple Mount. Before the Herodian era, the Temple Mount consisted of the Azarah Courtyard and the surrounding Har HaBayis Courtyard. Herod extended the boundaries of the Temple Mount. He surrounded the Har HaBayis Courtyard with a colonnade. The text discusses the probability that King Solomon may have built the eastern colonnade 800 years before Herod. Herod then constructed the Antonia Fortress to the north and the Royal Basilica to the south. This diagram is only an approximation of the various sections. Chapter 37 describes the attempt to establish a more accurate picture.

Plate 76. Floor plan of the Azarah
Courtesy: Eli Mayerfeld

KEY TO PLATE 76

1. soreg, fence
2. twelve steps
3. Women's Court Gate, Lower Gate
4. Women's Courtyard
5. Lower Court
6. Nazir's Chamber
7. Wood Chamber
8. Leper's Chamber
9. Oil Chamber
10. fifteen steps
11. Instrument Chamber
12. Nicanor Gate, Upper Gate
13. small gateways
14. Pinchus the Clothier's Chamber
15. High Priest's Meal Offering Chamber
16. Israelite Courtyard, duchan, platform
17. Priests' Courtyard
18. Supreme Court Chambers
19. High Priest's Chamber, Palhedron Chamber
20. Well Chamber
21. Salt Chamber
22. Parvah's Chamber, tannery
23. Rinser's Chamber
24. Water Gate, Avtinus Chamber, mikva
25. Firstborn Offering Gate
26. Firewood Gate
27. Upper Gate

28. Western Gates
29. Yechonia Gate, Spark Gate
30. Sacrifice Gate
31. Women's Gate
32. The Hearth, the Hearth Gate, Song Gate
33. Sheep Chamber
34. mikva entrance, Hearth Chamber
35. Showbread Chamber
36. Receipt Chamber
37. hooks, columns
38. tables
39. hoops
40. Altar
41. Shis, sewer
42. wash basin
43. twelve steps of the Heichel
44. Hall entrance
45. Hall
46. Knives Chamber
47. Kodesh, Heichel
48. Holy of Holies, Kodesh HaKadashim
49. small office entrance
50. small offices
51. ramp
52. Outer wall of Heichel
53. Water downpour area

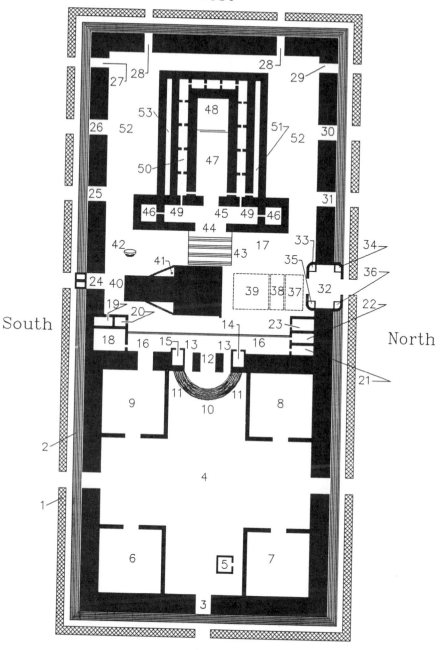

West

North

South

East

SCALE (in cubits)

0 10 25 ⊥ 50 75 100

The Cheil **79**

carrying on the Sabbath within the Temple courtyard, at least one new wall had to be built after the rooms had been constructed. The Soreg was fashioned after the inner rooms were built, thus carrying on the Sabbath was permitted within the courtyard (Rosh).

According to this view, the Soreg only needed to consist of one wall. That wall happened to be located 10 cubits in front of the Women's Courtyard, the eastern extension of the Azarah (see Plate 76). According to this view, the Soreg extended all the way from the northern Temple Mount wall to the southern Temple Mount wall.

However, according to most authorities, the Soreg completely surrounded the Azarah and Women's Courtyard. Non-Jews often came to the Holy Temple to offer prayers and to bring sacrifices. Only a burnt offering could be presented by a non-Jew. However, non-Jews were not permitted to enter the Azarah. The Soreg marked the point beyond which non-Jews could not pass. Stone markers, engraved in Greek and Latin, warned non-Jews not to pass beyond that point, lest they take their lives into their hands (*The Jewish War*, Book 5, chap. 5, para. 2). Two such marker stones have been found (Plate 77).

Jews who would be defiled by coming in contact with a corpse also could not pass beyond the Soreg (Tosfos Yom Tov quoting Ravyah).

Plate 77. A tablet with a warning in Greek forbidding non-Jews from entering the inner Sanctuary. It reads, "No gentile is allowed within the wall surrounding the sanctuary nor the enclosed courtyard. Anyone apprehended doing so is at the risk of taking his own life into his own hands."

Plate 78. The retaining wall that supports the Dome of the Rock platform (see Plate 114).

Some authorities picture the wooden Soreg as built atop a stone wall one cubit high (Tavnis Haichel). Other commentaries say that the Soreg was open only in the middle of the eastern side (Ravyah). Others believe it was open opposite all the doorways of the courtyard (Tiferes Yisroel).

When the Greeks invaded the Temple grounds in the pre-Hasmonean era, they broke open the Soreg in thirteen places. Their intention was either to make new openings or to widen preexisting openings. When the Hasmoneans regained the Temple, they repaired the Soreg. It was noticeable where the fence had been repaired, and the Sages issued a decree requiring the Temple worshipers to prostrate themselves upon encountering one of these repairs, as an act of praise to God for the miraculous recapture of the Temple (Midos 2:3).

The distance from the Soreg to the wall surrounding the inner courtyard was 10 cubits (a cubit is approximately one and a half feet). This 10-cubit space is called the Cheil. Four cubits of the Cheil were on level ground, and six cubits consisted of steps (see Plate 76, #2). There were twelve steps, each one half a cubit high and half a cubit deep. Some say the steps surrounded the entire courtyard on all four sides (Tiferes Yisroel). Others say it only surrounded the eastern section of the Azarah (Rashi, Yoma 16b).

The floor of the Women's Courtyard and the Azarah was elevated, and surrounded by a retaining wall. Maimonides says that the 10-cubit-high retaining wall (approximately 15 feet) was called the Cheil (Rambam, Bais HaB'chirah 2:2). All other rabbinic scholars apply the term Cheil to the area between the Soreg and the inner courtyard wall. According to them, the retaining wall had no specific name. Also, the height of the retaining wall (6 cubits) was equal to the height of the surrounding twelve steps.

The Dome of the Rock is built on an elevated platform. This is the only remnant of the elevated floor of the Holy Temple. This platform is surrounded by a 15-foot-high retaining wall. Perhaps it is the remains of the Maimonides Cheil (Plate 78). The platform of the Dome of the Rock will be discussed later.

17

The Women's Courtyard

The eastern section of the Azarah courtyard was called the Women's Courtyard (see Plate 76, #4). It was also called the Outer Courtyard, or the New Courtyard. Like all the courtyards, it was surrounded by a high wall 5 cubits thick (Tavnis Haichel). There were four gateways leading into this section. The one on the eastern side was called the Women's Courtyard Gate (see Plate 76, #3). It was also called the Lower Gate, or the Eastern Gate. Opposite this gateway, to the west, was the second gateway. Fifteen semicircular steps led up from the floor of the Women's Courtyard to this second gateway (Plate 76, #10), called the Upper Gate (Plate 76, #12). There was also one gate on the northern side and one gate on the southern side of the Women's Courtyard. All the gateways had gold-plated doors (Midos 2:3).

The Women's Courtyard was 135 cubits by 135 cubits (Midos 2:5). (As a rule, dimensions do not include the thickness of the wall.) Inside the Lower Gate, to the north, was another lower judicial court (see Plate 76, #5), over which twenty-three judges presided (Tiferes Yisroel).

The Women's Courtyard derived its name from the fact that women who came to the Temple assembled here. Some authorities maintain that they were not permitted beyond this area (Rashi, Kiddushin 52b). Others say that although women were permitted to pass beyond this section in order to offer their own sacrifices, they would return here immediately afterward (Tosfos).

During the festival of Tabernacles (Succos), the celebrated Rejoicing of the Water Drawing Ceremony (Simchas Bais HaSho'ava) was held in the Women's Courtyard. Originally, the women assembled in the courtyard and the men danced and sang outside, beyond the Cheil. Since the women were unable to have a good view from inside the Women's Courtyard, they would pass beyond the doors into that area. The mingling of men and women during a sacred celebration was not permitted; therefore, to remedy the situation, the festivities were held inside the Women's Courtyard. During the festival, the north and south gates were blocked and balconies were erected to provide a viewing area for the women (Succah 51a, Tiferes Yisroel). The fact that the Holy Temple had a separate section for women is the source of the women's section or gallery in a synagogue (Igres Moshe).

In each of the four corners of the Women's Courtyard were large, unroofed rooms (Midos 2:5), each 40 cubits by 40 cubits (Tiferes Yisroel). However, according to Chanukas HaBayis, from east to west was 40 cubits, from north to south, 30 cubits.

The chamber in the southeastern corner was the Chamber of the Nazirites (see Plate 76, #6). Upon completion of the Nazirite pledge, the Nazirite would offer three sacrifices, a burnt offering ("olah"), a sin offering ("chatas"), and a peace offering ("shlamim"). The peace offering was cooked in the Chamber of the Nazirites. The Nazirite's hair was shorn and the clippings tossed into the fire over which the peace offering was cooking.

The northeastern room was called the Chamber of the Wood (see Plate 76, #7). The wood used for burning the sacrifices on top of the Altar was sorted in this chamber. Elderly priests and those unqualified to perform the Temple service sorted the wood here. Any wood that was rotting or worm-infested was unfit for the Altar. However, the priests were permitted to use the unfit wood to cook the sacrificial meat, which was theirs to eat.

The Talmud records the following incident. It once happened that priests were sitting and sorting wood in the Chamber of the Wood, when one of them noticed that a floor tile was loose. He realized that this led to the secret passage in which the Holy Ark was hidden. The Ark had been hidden during the time of Josiah (Yoshiyahu) toward the end of the First Temple era. When the Jews returned from the seventy-year exile, the Ark could not be found. Tradition says that there was to be no Ark during the Second Temple era. This priest, who had discovered the hidden place of the Ark, sought to crack open the tile with his hatchet, when suddenly fire issued forth and consumed him. This was taken as an omen that the Ark should remain hidden (Shekalim 6:1).

The room in the northwestern corner was the Chamber of the Lepers ("m'tzorah" is often mistranslated as "leper," but since no known modern-day disease symptomatic of a m'tzorah is known, the term leper will have to suffice) (see Plate 76, #8). After being healed of "leprosy," the former leper would immerse himself in a mikva located in this chamber. Afterward, he would offer the purification sacrifices (Midos 2:5).

The fourth room in the Women's Courtyard was in the southwestern corner. It was called the Chamber of Oils (see Plate 76, #9). In this room the oil, wine, and flour needed for sacrificial purposes were stored. Generally, if one wanted to offer a sacrifice, he had first to purchase the animal on his own outside the Temple grounds. The street along the Tyropean Way was crowded with cattle dealers for this very purpose. However, if one wished to present a meal offering (mincha), the necessary ingredients could be purchased in the Holy Temple. The purchaser would first go to the Chamber of the Receipts (see Plate 76, #36). He would explain to the attendant the type of meal offering he required. He would then pay for it, and the attendant would hand over a receipt listing his purchases. The receipt would be taken to the Chamber of Oils and that attendant would dispense the required amounts of oil, wine, and flour. The ingredients were presented to a priest in the main courtyard, and the priest would prepare the offering.

Of the four chambers, three had only one doorway, leading from the Women's Courtyard into the room. The Chamber of Oils, however, had two doorways. One led into the room from the Women's Courtyard, and the other led into the room from the main courtyard, which was to the west of the Women's Courtyard (Tosefta, Yoma 1:3). While most authorities say that these four chambers were located within the Women's Courtyard, another opinion states that they were located outside the courtyard (Rosh).

At the western end of the Women's Courtyard were fifteen semicircular steps (see Plate 76, #10) (Midos 2:5). Each was half a cubit high and half a cubit deep. On occasion, the Levites sang as they stood on these steps. The steps were called the Ascents of Song (Shiur HaMa'alos). Psalms contains fifteen Songs of Ascent.

Near the base of the steps, built into the western wall of the Women's Courtyard, were two doors that led underneath the Azarah, which was built on higher ground than the Women's Courtyard. The doors led into a single large underground chamber called the Chamber of the Instruments (see Plate 76, #11). Here the Levites conducted choir rehearsals and stored their instruments. There was another underground passageway that led from the Chamber of the Instruments under the northern wall of the main courtyard (Midos 2:6, Tiferes Yisroel).

18

The Courtyard
of the Israelites

The doorway atop the fifteen semicircular steps led into the Azarah. The first eleven cubits along the eastern side of the Azarah were called the Courtyard of the Israelites (Plate 79).

The gateway atop the fifteen steps that led into the Courtyard of the Israelites were called the Upper Gate, also known as the Nicanor Gate (see Plate 76, #12).

Nicanor was the benefactor who paid craftsmen in Alexandria, Egypt, to fashion two large brass doors. Each door was 5 cubits by 20 cubits. The brass was carved with intricate designs, and its finish was exceedingly bright. As these doors were being sent by ship from Egypt to Judea, a storm broke out. The crew realized they had no choice but to cast overboard one of the two brass doors. When the ship docked, to everyone's amazement the door cast overboard was found floating in the harbor (Yoma 3:8).

All the Temple doors were plated with gold except the Nicanor Gate. The rabbis wanted the people to see the "miracle doors" in their pristine form, and, besides, the brass finish had the appearance of fine gold (Midos 2:3).

These heavy doors required twenty men to open them. The Nicanor Gate was opened only on the Sabbath, festivals, and the New Moon. If the king was present in the Temple, the doors were also opened in his honor (Tavnis Haichel).

There were two smaller gateways to the left and right of the Nicanor Gate (see Plate 76, #13). These were the gates used for

Plate 79. The Nicanor Gate, which led up from the Women's Courtyard to the Courtyard of the Israelites.

entrance into the Courtyard of the Israelites (Rosh). (However, the Shiltai HaGiborim says that the two smaller doors were built into the large doors.)

In ancient times, any wife accused of committing adultery was brought to the Temple and given a drink of "bitter waters." If she survived the ordeal, it was taken to be a sign of her innocence (Numbers 5:11–31). The drinking of the bitter waters by the unfaithful wife was performed inside the small gate to the north. Healed lepers and women who had given birth would also stand inside that gateway while their sacrifices were offered (Sota 7a).

Generally, the space contained within a doorway of the courtyard had the same sanctity as the courtyard itself. The one exception was the Nicanor Gate. The space within the doorway only had the sanctity of the Women's Courtyard. A person who had become defiled by coming in contact with a corpse was forbidden by rabbinical decree from passing beyond the Soreg into the Women's Courtyard. However, it was forbidden by Torah law for that person to enter the Courtyard of the Israelites (Rambam, Bais HaB'chirah, 3:12).

To the north and south of the Nicanor Gate, inside the Courtyard of the Israelites, were two chambers. To the north was the Chamber of Pinchas the Clothier (see Plate 76, #14) (Midos 1:4). Pinchas was a renowned clothier who catered to the priests (Rambam, Kli HaMikdash 7:5). The attendants in this chamber not only fashioned the priestly garments, but also assisted in dressing the priests for the Temple service (Shiltai HaGiborim).

There were ninety-six cubicles for storing the priestly vestments. There were twenty-four priestly divisions, and four types of priestly garments: trousers, a shirt, a belt, and a turban. Each priestly division had four cubicles for garment storage (Tavnis Haichel).

To the south of the Nicanor Gate was the Chamber of the High Priest's Meal Offering (Plate 76, #15) (Midos 1:4). Every day twelve meal offerings (minchas chavitim) had to be brought, paid for by the High Priest. The meal offerings were prepared for the High Priest in this chamber. Half were offered upon the Altar in the morning and half in the afternoon. Some commentators say that these two rooms, the Chamber of Pinchas the Clothier and the Chamber of the High Priest's Meal Offering, were built into the wall (Chanukas HaBayis).

The length of the Courtyard of the Israelites from north to south was 135 cubits. Its width was 11 cubits. Israelites remained in their courtyard while their sacrifices were offered by the priests. If conditions were crowded, the Israelites were permitted to go beyond their courtyard.

In the Courtyard of the Israelites was a throne for the king, to be used when he attended the Temple service. The throne was elevated and supported by two columns 20 cubits high and 4 cubits thick. The seat above was protected by a beautifully decorated canopy, and gold embroidered curtains surrounded the throne (Tavnis Haichel).

Rising from the Courtyard of the Israelites into the next courtyard were four steps called the duchan (Plate 76, #16). The duchan steps went across the entire width of the courtyard (Midos 2:6).

Surrounding the entire Azarah courtyard was a colonnade,

columns supporting a roof. On display in the courtyard were the spoils of war, as praise to God who granted His nation the strength to overpower and overcome those who sought to destroy them and His Holy House (Tavnis Haichel).

19

The Azarah Courtyard and Its Gateways

Leading up from the Courtyard of the Israelites into the main section of the Temple courtyard were the four duchan steps. The bottom step was one cubit high and half a cubit deep. This was the only Temple step with a height of more than half a cubit. The remaining steps of the duchan were half a cubit high and half a cubit deep (Plate 76, #16). The duchan stretched across the Azarah, and on these steps the Levites would sing psalms twice each day. When the priests blessed the people, they would stand on the steps of the main building in the Temple, called the Heichel (Plate 76, #43). If so many priests were present that the steps in front of the Heichel could not accommodate them, the priests would move to the duchan and the Levites would stand on the fifteen steps that led up from the Women's Courtyard (Plate 76, #10).

The courtyard, from the Nicanor Gate to its western wall, was called the Azarah. The holiest sacrifices could be eaten only in this area. In the southern wall of the Azarah were four gateways. In the northern wall there were also four gateways. On the western wall there were two. On the eastern wall was the Nicanor Gate.

On the southern wall, the first gateway toward the east, was the Water Gate (Plate 76, #24) (Midos 2:6). This gateway, like all the other large gateways, was 10 cubits wide and 20 cubits high (Midos 2:3), and also like the other large gateways, had a beautifully embroidered curtain (Rambam, Kli HaMikdash 7:17). It was called Water Gate for several reasons. During the festival of Tabernacles (Succos), the priests drew water from the Shiloach Brook and brought it into the Azarah through this gateway. The water was carried amid much pomp and ceremony. The pitcher of water was poured on top of the Altar (Plate 76, #40) together with a pitcher of wine. This festival began five days after Yom Kippur and lasted for seven days. This ritual showed that before God the water was equal to the wine, representing the equality of all men after the Day of Atonement. The Water Gate gateway was open only during the festival (Tiferes Yisroel).

The Water Gate took its name as well from the narrow stream of water that flowed from beneath the foundations of the Heichel (Plate 76, #47), across the courtyard, and out through the Water Gate (Yoma 77b).

Outside the Water Gate above the gateway were two rooms. The western room was called the Avtinus Chamber (Plate 76, #24) (Tiferes Yisroel). In this room the incense that was offered on the Golden Altar was compounded. The chamber was named after an illustrious family of spice makers. They knew of a certain ingredient, which, when added to the incense, made the smoke rise in a straight column. They refused to divulge the name of this ingredient lest others use it for idol worship (Yoma 38a).

During the Second Temple period, the High Priesthood was a political appointment based on reasons other than merit. Often the High Priest was unable to read Hebrew. The aristocrats who were selected to serve as High Priests led such isolated lives that they did not know the difference between an ox and a goat. One week before Yom Kippur, the High Priest was taught how to perform the Temple Service for the Holy Day of Atonement. It was in the Chamber of Avtinus that he was taught how to present the special Yom Kippur incense offering, which was burned in the Holy of Holies (Rashi, Yoma 19a).

The Talmud mentions the Katrus family among the priestly officers (Pesachim 57a). Katrus family members served either as successors or assistants to the Avtinus family. Their family home was recently discovered in the Old City of Jerusalem (Plate 80), in the Upper City. In the room in the house used for compounding the spices, all the utensils and the table were made of stone. Stone is not susceptible to defilement. The house had its own mikva. The stone weights and many of the original utensils are still there (Plate 81). A month after the Romans burned the Holy Temple in 70 C.E.,

Plate 81.   A Roman spear found in the Bar Katrus house.

Plate 80.   The ruins of the Bar Katrus house. Located in the Upper City, the house was destroyed about one month after the destruction of the Temple by the Romans.

they set fire to the Upper City. The walls of the Katrus's house still show signs of scorching.

A Roman spear was also found there. The remains of a young woman's arm, found leaning against the base of the kitchen wall, gives testimony to the brutality our ancestors suffered during their final hours.

The chamber next to the Avtinus Chamber above the Water Gate was a mikva. It was used only once during the entire year, by the High Priest on Yom Kippur. On that Holy Day, the High Priest immersed himself five times in a mikva. The first immersion was done here (Yoma 30a). This mikva, above the Water Gate, may also have contributed to the gate's name.

To the west of the Water Gate was the Gate of the Firstborn Offering (Plate 76, #25) (Midos 2:6). Sacrifices are divided into two types: those of greater and those of lesser sanctity. Those of greater sanctity had to be slaughtered north of the Altar. Those of lesser sanctity could be slaughtered anywhere in the Azarah, even in the southern area. The firstborn offering was one of the more common sacrifices of lesser sanctity and was therefore brought in through a southern gate to indicate its minor sanctity (Tiferes Yisroel). Some say that when Abraham brought Isaac, his firstborn, to be sacrificed upon the mount, he passed this way (Rosh).

The next gateway to the west was the Gate of the Firewood (Plate 76, #26) (Midos 2:6). The forests of Jerusalem were located west of the Upper City. The wood was cut down and brought in through the Kiphonus Gate, the only gate on the western side of the Temple Wall to lead directly onto the Temple Mount. The wood could not be brought in through any of the western gates surrounding the Azarah, because those gates were much narrower and smaller than the others. The wood had to be carried around to the southern part of the Azarah and brought in through one of those gateways, which was called the Gate of the Firewood. Although there was a closer gate, which we will discuss next, it, too, was a small gateway (Chanukas HaBayis). The firewood from the Wood Chamber (Plate 76, #7) was also brought into the Azarah through the Gate of the Firewood (Tosfos Yeshanim, Yoma 19a).

The last gate on the southern wall of the Azarah was the Upper Gate (Plate 76, #27), not to be confused with the Nicanor Gate that was also called the Upper Gate (Midos 2:6). The gateway of which we speak now was the highest point on the Temple Mount (Tiferes Yisroel). It was narrower than the other three along the southern wall (Tosfos, Kesubos 106a).

Along the northern wall of the Azarah were four gateways. The first was called the Song Gate (Plate 76, #32) (Midos 2:6). The Levites would bring their musical instruments through this gateway (Tosfos Yom Tov). This first gate on the northern wall is also called the Hearth Gate (Midos 1:4). The lodging room for the priests was in a building called the Hearth (Plate 76, #32). It was the only heated building in the Temple and as heat was only needed at night, the one room used at night was their lodge. Underground was a large fireplace or hearth, with pipes conducting the heat upstairs which is why the lodge was known as the Hearth. The Hearth was built into the northern wall of the Azarah. The gateway leading from the Cheil into the Hearth was called the Hearth Gate. The question is how the first gate could be both the Song Gate and the Hearth Gate. Admittedly, one gateway could have two names. The Nicanor Gate had many names (Eruvin 5:1). However, in this case it cannot be. Why would the Levites bring their musical instruments into the Temple through the sleeping quarters of the priests? This problem will be resolved later when we discuss the Hearth.

The next gateway, to the west along the northern wall of the Azarah, was the Women's Gate (Plate 76, #31) (Midos 2:6). Women would stand in this gateway while their sacrifice was being offered (Tiferes Yisroel). This, too, was a smaller gateway (Tosfos, Kesubos 106a).

The next northern gateway was called the Sacrifice Gate (Plate 76, #30) (Midos 2:6). Through this gate the animals that had greater sanctity and had to be slaughtered north of the Altar were brought (Chanukas HaBayis). Why wasn't this called the Greater Sanctity Gate? Because if one pledged to bring a sacrifice and did not specify whether it would be of greater or lesser sanctity, he must bring a burnt offering, which is a greater sanctity sacrifice. The name of the gateway teaches us this law, reminding us that an unspecified sacrifice implies a greater sanctity sacrifice.

The last gateway along the northern wall had two names. It was called the Gate of Joachim and the Gate of Sparks (Plate 76, #29) (Midos 1:5, 2:6). It was called the Gate of Joachim because it was from this very spot that King Joachim was led into exile by Nebuchadnezzar toward the end of the First Temple era (Tiferes Yisroel). Later, it was called the Gate of Sparks. Next to the gateway was a small courtyard surrounded by columns, which supported a balcony upon which a priestly guard—twenty-four priests and Levites—stood watch at night. The sun's rays shining between the columns appeared to be flickering sparks, giving the gate its name (Rosh). Inside the small courtyard was a pile of constantly burning coals. This provided a source of fire, whenever it was needed. This pile of coals gave off sparks and embers, which others say may be the source of the name Gate of Sparks (B'air Sheva).

The balcony upon which the priests stood guard had a staircase that led down to the Cheil outside the Azarah (Midos 1:5). Some say the small courtyard was located in the Azarah itself (Tiferes Yisroel). Others say it was located in the Cheil (Rav). Still others maintain that part of it was built in front of the gate, and part behind it (HaM'forash to Tamid 1:1).

The two gates on the western side were small doorways that had no names (Plate 76, #28) (Midos 2:6). One was located toward the south and the other was located toward the north (Tiferes Yisroel).

The Mishna (Midos 2:6) says, ". . . two gates of the Azarah were on the western wall . . . they had no name." It is most peculiar that the Mishna would have to tell us that something had no name. The Mishna text should simply have stated, ". . . and there were two gateways on the western wall." Second, why did these two gateways have no name? Every other gateway had a name. Third, in the Holy Temple diagram of the commentary Kaftor V'ferach, there are no gates on the western side. How can we account for this oversight?

The Dome of the Rock is built on an elevated platform. This elevation was made by Herod. However, the platform is trapezoidal (see Plate 36). Why would Herod build it in such an awkward shape? It is true that the wall surrounding the Temple Mount that was also built by King Herod is trapezoidal. However, those walls, which are Herod's extension, merely follow the contour of the mountain's slope. What can account for the peculiar shape of the Dome's platform?

In *Antiquities* (Book 15, chap. 11, para. 3) Josephus writes, ". . . but twenty cubits of the [Herodian] foundation fell down." How can a foundation fall down? Josephus tells us that it was never repaired. How can the Temple be built and stand on a fallen foundation? In *The Jewish War* Josephus writes, ". . . war towers were built and stationed behind the western wall [of the Azarah] because there were no steps there, but on the other sides there were steps." Why were there no steps on the western side? The Azarah was elevated. How would one descend these nameless western gates to the Cheil without steps?

Josephus tells us that Herod sought to elevate the Azarah "twenty cubits." He did this by constructing a platform, upon which the Dome of the Rock is constructed. This platform Josephus calls the "foundation." Parts of the foundation fell in. Due to some construction problem, Herod was not able to built up the western sector of the foundation, so steps were never built there. Likewise, the gateways of the Western Wall were never rebuilt. Herod intended to wait until the elevated platform or "foundation" was fixed on the western side before building the steps and two gateways. The foundation was never completely fixed, so the two gateways were never rebuilt. Perhaps this is the reading of the Mishna text, "lo haya lahem *sham*" (instead of "shem"), "the two western gateways they did not have *there*." Although the two doorways were present in the pre-Herodian Temple, they did not exist during the Herodian rebuilding due to construction problems in that sector.

Chambers
of the Courtyard

In the Azarah were several buildings, rooms, and chambers. The Supreme Court Chamber (Plate 76, #18), also called the Chamber of Cut Stone, was one of these buildings (Midos 5:4). Its location is disputed. Our Mishna text says that it was located in the south; however, there are existing texts that put it in the north. Most authorities do place it in the northern wall. Some say that it was on the northern wall of the Azarah toward the east (Tiferes Yisroel). Others say that it was toward the west (Tavnis Haichel).

The Supreme Court Building was half within the Azarah and half outside, in the Cheil. There were doors leading from the chamber to the Azarah and doors leading to the Cheil. It had to be located partially in the Cheil because judges had to be seated when deciding legal matters. Only the king was permitted to sit in the Azarah, and then only if he was of Davidic descent. The judges therefore would sit in the portion of the chamber located in the Cheil. The chamber was located partially within the Azarah because the section of the Torah that deals with the judicial system also contains the laws pertaining to the Azarah (Deuteronomy 16).

It was called the Chamber of the Cut Stone because of the material used to build it (Tosfos Yom Tov). Also, in Hebrew, to render a legal decision is called "p'sak," which literally means "to cut" or "to decide" (Rabaynu Bechayah, Deuteronomy 1:17).

The Talmud says that the Supreme Court Chamber was a basilica

(Yoma 25a), a type of architecture described in the section on the Royal Basilica.

Adjoining the Supreme Court Chamber was the Chamber of the High Priest (Plate 76, #19) (Midos 5:4). For the first half of the Second Temple era, this chamber was called the Belutai Chamber. Belutai was a type of Roman official who held office for life. Later the room was called the Palhedron, or Parhedron, Chamber, after a Roman official who held office for twelve months. During the Hasmonean and Herodian periods, a priest could buy the High Priesthood. After a year, another priest would buy it (Yoma 8b).

The Chamber of the High Priest was also called the Wood Room. Many interpretations are offered as to the source of this name. One says that wood is different from stone. Stone can last forever even if it is not taken care of. Wood requires care or it will deteriorate and rot. The High Priest was expected to take care that his deeds and thoughts befitted a man of his station; otherwise, he would not last (Tiferes Yisroel).

Another version says that the High Priest's garments were stored in the room (Rambam, Kli HaMikdash 8:10) in wooden chests; hence the name Wood Chamber (Tavnis Haichel). Others say the room was occupied by the High Priest only on the week before Yom Kippur, and for the remainder of the year the room was used for wood storage (Kesef Mishna). Another opinion is that the name of the room was a blessing to the High Priest—may his reign be long like the years of a tree (Tosfos Chadashim). Still others say that the room was located near the Firewood Gate (Tavnis Haichel). Just as there is a difference of opinion about where the Supreme Court Chamber was, whether it was on the northern or the southern wall, so there is a difference of opinion regarding this chamber, which was connected to the Supreme Court Chamber.

One last opinion as to the derivation of Wood Chamber: The chamber of the High Priest was built out of wood rather than stone (Tosfos Yom Tov quoting Raavad). Why was this the only building to be made of wood? Since it was used only one week out of the year, during the High Holy Days, perhaps it was not a permanent feature of the Temple and was built anew each year (Kesef Mishna).

Seven days before Yom Kippur, the High Priest would leave his mansion and family in the Upper City and take up residence in this chamber. He would be instructed in the Yom Kippur service by the Supreme Court members and by the priestly scholars (Yoma 2a).

This was the only room in the Holy Temple to have a mezuzah. Although by law no Temple room is required to have one, the sages did not want the High Priest to feel as though he were living in a prison cell, which does not require a mezuzah (Yoma 10a).

There is disagreement among the commentaries about whether the High Priest's chamber was built inside or outside the Azarah. If it was built inside, how could the High Priest sit down, since sitting was not permitted in the Azarah? And how could he sleep there? The solution offered is that the door to the chamber was located outside the Azarah in the Cheil. The ruling was that if any room, even one inside the Azarah, had a door opening only to the outside of the Azarah, then the room itself was considered outside (Tosfos Yom Tov). Others believe the opposite, that the chamber was built outside the Azarah, but the entrance was inside. However, the ruling also states that a chamber outside the Azarah whose entrance is located in the Azarah is considered part of the Azarah. How then could the priest sleep there? The solution proposed is that although a room located outside the Azarah, but whose entrance is located within, is considered within the Azarah, that ruling is only with regard to eating sacred meat. Only concerning eating is that room part of the Azarah, but not with regard to the restriction of sitting or sleeping (Tosfos, Yoma 8b).

Another room in the Azarah was the Chamber of the Well (Plate 76, #20) (Midos 4:5). A waterwheel supplied a quick drink for a thirsty priest (Tavnis Haichel). This room was paid for by Jews who lived outside Israel, called the Exiled Jews or the Goleh. The Hebrew name for the Chamber of the Well was the Goleh Chamber (Rav). Goleh can also mean a large tank. Every morning a large tank was filled with well water for the priests (Tiferes Yisroel). These three rooms, the Supreme Court Chamber, the High Priest's Chamber, and the Chamber of the Well, formed one building (Midos 4:5).

Across from that building, on the wall opposite the Azarah, was another building complex. It, too, consisted of three chambers. The first was called the Salt Chamber (Plate 76, #21) (Midos 5:3) as this was where salt was stored. Every sacrifice offered first had to be salted. The ramp leading to the top of the Altar was sprinkled with salt so no one would slip. On the roof of the Salt Chamber was a terrace on which the priests ate their portion of the sacrificial meat (Tavnis Haichel).

Next to the Salt Chamber was the Parvah Chamber (Plate 76, #22) (Midos 5:3). The leather from the sacrifices with a greater degree of sanctity (kodshai kodoshim) belonged to the priests. It was taken into the Parvah Chamber to be salted and preserved (Tiferes Yisroel). On top was a mikva, used four times on Yom Kippur by the High Priest (Yoma 3:3). The structure was built by a man named Parvah, a practitioner of witchcraft. He tried to dig a tunnel from under the Parvah Chamber into the Holy of Holies to watch the High Priest secretly on Yom Kippur. He was found, and killed in the Parvah Chamber (Rambam). Some opinions maintain that the Parvah Chamber was below ground, and the mikva on top was level with the Azarah (Tosfos, Yoma 31a).

The third room of this complex was the Rinser's Chamber (Plate 76, #23). In this room the internal organs of the sacrifice were soaked and rinsed (Midos 5:3). From the roof of the Rinser's Chamber was an access route to the mikva on top of the Parvah Chamber, by ramp (Tiferes Yisroel) or a circular staircase (Rav).

Some maintain that the Rinser's Chamber was also below ground level (Tosfos, Yoma 31a).

<h1 style="text-align:right">21</h1>

<h1 style="text-align:center">The Hearth</h1>

The largest building in the Azarah was the Heichel, which will be discussed later. The second largest was the Hearth (Plate 76, #32). This dome-covered structure was the sleeping quarters for the priests who performed the services (Midos 1:6–9).

One opinion locates the Hearth right outside the Azarah (Rambam, Bais HaB'chirah 2:9). Most authorities say that it was half inside the Azarah and half outside (Rosh). It was built on the northern wall, and had four side rooms connected with the structure. Some say that the side rooms were outside the building (Rosh, Tosfos, Yoma 15b, 17b). Others say that the four side rooms were inside the building, one room in each corner (Tiferes Yisroel).

The Hearth itself served as a dormitory. The walls were lined with great stone steps. Some sources say the priests slept on these steps (Rav), while others maintain that the sleeping quarters were built into the wall, like cubicles or coops. The priests would climb the steps to their respective cubicles (B'air Sheva). The elder priests slept above, and the younger ones slept on the floor (Midos). Although most authorities say that the priests could only sleep in the section of the Hearth that was outside the Azarah (HaM'forash to Tamid), one rabbinic source allowed the priests to sleep even within the confines of the Temple courtyard, as sleep was necessary for them to perform the service properly (Raavad).

In the middle of the floor was a tile one cubit by one cubit. It could be raised by lifting a hoop set into it. Underneath was a chain, to which were attached the keys to the gates. One of the priestly officials would take the keys after the Temple doors were locked at night, place them on the chain, and sleep atop the tile (Midos 1:9).

The Hearth had two doors. One led into the Cheil and the other led into the Azarah. The door that led into the Azarah had a smaller door next to it (Rosh). Some say that this smaller door was built into the large one (Rav, Tamid 3:1). The small door was used early in the morning. Many priests were needed to open the large door and in the early morning hours only a few were awake. We learn that it took twenty priests to open the Nicanor Gates.

As stated earlier, four rooms were connected to the Hearth. One was to the southwest, called the Sheep Chamber (Plate 76, #33) (Midos 1:6). It was a stable that could hold at least eight sheep. Whenever animals were needed for sacrifices, they were purchased in the markets of Jerusalem and used that day. Every day of the year two special sacrifices were offered. One was called the Morning Tamid—the first sacrifice of the day. The other was the Afternoon Tamid, the last sacrifice of the day. These two sacrifices were unique. The animals had to be examined and checked for blemishes and imperfections twice every day for four days before they could be used. Thus, because the Holy Temple had to have a supply of animals on hand, these animals were kept in the Sheep Chamber. The stone walls of the rooms and chambers prevented any odors from passing into the main section of the Hearth. The Sheep Chamber was also called the Sacrifice Chamber (Rosh).

The room to the southeast was called the Chamber of the Showbread (Plate 76, #35). Every Friday, twelve showbreads were baked in the chamber, and on the Sabbath they were placed on the Golden Table in the Kodesh (Plate 76, #47) (Midos 1:6).

The northeastern room was called the Receipt Chamber (Tamid 3:3) (Plate 76, #36), where the meal offering was paid for. We discussed this room earlier in the description of the Chamber of the Oils.

When the Maccabees regained the Temple, they disassembled the Altar. It had been defiled by the Syrian–Greeks and their pagan sacrifices. A new Altar was built and the old one was stored beneath the Receipt Chamber (Midos 1:6). It is interesting to note that the Altar was 81,000 cubic feet. To store it required a room 10 feet high and 90 feet long by 90 feet wide. Looking at the diagram of the Receipt Chamber, it is obvious that the basement must have been many times larger than the chamber itself.

The fourth room, located in the northwest, was the Hearth Chamber (Plate 76, #34). In this room was a ramp (Rav) or spiral staircase (HaM'forash on Tamid) going down beneath the ground to the mikva and bathrooms (Midos 1:6, Tamid 1:1). The underground passageway led under the Cheil and under the Antonia Fortress northward. The walls had niches cut into them in which oil lamps were placed to give light in these dark tunnels (Tamid 1:1).

There was more than one tunnel under the Azarah. The first one, as described, led under the Antonia to the priests' mikva. The second came from the northern side of the Holy Temple and led into the Chamber of Instruments. A third tunnel led under the Kodesh (Pesachim 86a). It is very likely that all these tunnels were interconnected, and that a doorway in the northern side of the Cheil led to this system of tunnels. That doorway had two names. It was referred to as the Song Gate because it led to the tunnel that in turn led to the Chamber of Instruments, and it was also called the Hearth Gate because it led to the mikva, which had a fireplace, and then upstairs to the priests' quarters (the Hearth). It is interesting to note that one opinion in the Talmud even allowed the fireplace to be lit on the Sabbath (Rav Huna, Shabbos 19b).

One authority envisioned the Hearth as an underground vaulted structure. That opinion translated the word "dome" to mean "vaults." According to that opinion, the roof of the Hearth was level with the floor of the Azarah, and upon it stood a priestly guard (HaM'forash to Tamid).

Today, under the platform on which the Dome of the Rock stands are the remains of a series of underground tunnels (Plate 35). One, called cistern number 1, leads from the north, straight toward the rock. A second tunnel, called cistern number 3, branches off to the west. The significance of these archeological remains will be discussed at the conclusion of the section on the Altar.

22

The Altar

The area from the Courtyard of the Israelites to the front wall of the Heichel (Plate 87, #47) was called the Courtyard of the Priests (Plate 76, #17). The focal point of this courtyard was the Altar (Plate 76, #40).

The Altar consisted of three platforms, stacked to form a pyramid. A series of ramps led up from the southern side to the top. The Altar was made of small stones, lime, pitch, and glazing (Tiferes Yisroel). The stones were perfectly smooth, with no nicks or scratches that could be detected with the thumbnail. These stones were never touched by metal, because metal is believed to shorten the life of man, and the Altar represents the lengthening of life (Midos 3:4).

Most commentaries understand the Mishna to mean that metal is used in instruments of war, which shorten man's life. However, it can be argued that metal is used in all kinds of other instruments that bring comfort to life. In the early biblical epoch men lived extended lives, hundreds of years long. One of the commentators (Seder HaDoros) says that because men lacked tools, tasks took much longer. Without a metal plow, it could take years to cultivate a field. Therefore, it was necessary to live such long lives. With the advent of metal tools, introduced by Noah, men could accomplish the same tasks in a much shorter time. There was no longer a need for extended lives. Perhaps that is the intention of the Mishna, "metal shortens the life of man."

The stones used in the Altar were dug from deep beneath the earth's surface and were taken from virgin soil. Some were brought from beneath river beds, to ensure that metal never touched them (Midos 2:3). Stones used in the construction of the rest of the Temple were also smooth; however, the regulations concerned with coming into contact with metal were different. The stones could be worked with metal, but not on the Temple grounds (Tamid 26b). Even so, should the stones come into contact with metal, they could still be used. However, after the Altar was built, its stones could not be touched by metal. If any were, they had to be replaced (Kesef Mishna, Bais HaB'chirah 14:15).

All the structures on Har HaBayis rested on an elevated floor, with the exception of the Altar, which came in direct contact with the mountain's rock (Rambam, Bais HaB'chirah 1:13).

Stones could not have any perceptible scratches. If a single stone came loose from the Altar, the Altar was not fit for ritual use until it was repaired. The plaster coating on the Altar did not have to be perfectly smooth. If a piece of plaster, up to the size of an olive (or some say the size of a fist [tefach]), came loose, the Altar was still fit for use (Chullin 18a).

The Altar consisted of three platforms (Plate 82). The bottom one was called the Foundation. It was 32 cubits long, 32 cubits wide and 5/6 of a cubit high (Rambam, Bais HaB'chirah. 2:7. According to the Rav it was 1 cubit high. The Tosfos Yom Tov, in his commentary on Ezekiel, Tzuras HaBayis, says the Foundation was 2 cubits high.). It did not have the shape of a perfect square, because part of it was missing. There are various opinions as to the shape of the missing section and its dimensions (Plate 83).

The second platform was called the Sovayv ("around"—it was possible to walk around the roof of this platform, but not around that of the Foundation). It was 30⅓ cubits long, 30⅓ cubits wide

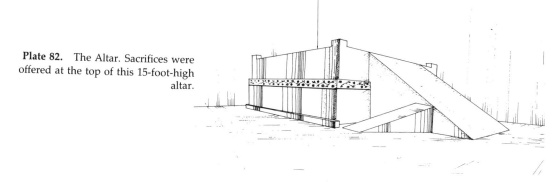

Plate 82. The Altar. Sacrifices were offered at the top of this 15-foot-high altar.

To Scale

Plate 83. Three opinions on the base of the Altar.

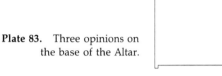

According to the Tosafos Yom Tov

According to the Vilna Gaon

According to Maimonides in his commentary to the Mishna

and 5 cubits high (Rambam; however, according to Rashi it was 30 by 30 by 5 cubits). Because on occasion the priests had to walk around the roof of the Sovayv, there was a small wall built on the edge to prevent them from falling off (Tiferes Yisroel).

The upper platform was called the Place of Arrangement. On top of this platform the stacks of burning lumber were arranged. This platform was 28⅔ cubits long, 28⅔ cubits wide, and 3 cubits high (Rambam; however, according to the Rav the dimensions were 28 by 28 by 3).

Built on the four corners of the top platform were four cornerstones whose dimensions were 1 cubit long, 1 cubit wide, and ⅚ of a cubit high. These cornerstones were hollow (Rambam). Some say that they were set back from the edge of the top platform ⅓ of a cubit (Raavad).

Around the top of the platform was a trench in which the priests stood when working on top of the Altar. The trench was a cubit deep. Some authorities say that the trench started near the edge of the top platform and was 2 cubits wide (Rashi, Zevachim 62b). Others say it was only 1 cubit wide and located 2 cubits from the edge (Rambam).

One commentator maintains that there was another platform resting on top of the Place of Arrangement. That platform was 22 cubits by 22 cubits and 1 cubit high (Raavad).

On top of the Altar, in the center, was a large pile of ash. This was the accumulated remains of the sacrifices, and was used to show to what extent the Altar was being used. It was called the Apple, because of its large, fruit-like shape. (In Hebrew it was called tapu'ach, which Tosfos, Shabbos 77a says means large fruit, not necessarily apple, and more probably refers to a citron or esrog.)

Also on top of the Altar were two basins, built onto the southwestern portion of the Place of Arrangement. They were used on the Festival of Tabernacles for the Water Drawing Ceremony.

There were several piles of burning lumber on the top of the Altar. One was called the Large Arrangement. It was east of the Apple and the sacrifices were burned on it. The wood used was usually walnut, pine, or fig. Actually any wood could be used, although the practice was not to use olive wood or grapevine. Two reasons are given: First, their products, olive oil and grapes (wine), were used on the Altar; therefore, they didn't have to give of "themselves." A second reason is that olives and grapes were important commodities in Israel. The Rabbis did not want anyone to cut down an olive tree or grapevine that was still productive. To discourage it, they made a rule that no olive wood or grapevine would be used in the Temple (Tamid 2:3, Tavnis Haichel).

Wood was cut from the forests from the month of Nissan (March–April) until the Fifteenth of Av (July–August). On the Fifteenth of Av, a celebration was held called Breaking the Saw (Tavnis Haichel).

A second pile of lumber was set aside on the top of the Altar as fuel for the burning of the incense. The incense was offered twice each day on the Golden Altar, which stood in the Heichel.

A third pile of lumber atop the Altar was used by the priests as they performed the commandment of igniting the Altar each day. Actually, one of the other two piles of lumber could have been used for this purpose. On Yom Kippur a special pile was set aside as fire for the burning of the incense in the Holy of Holies (Yoma 4:5).

The blood of certain sacrifices had to be touched to the upper half of the wall of the Altar. The blood of other sacrifices had to be poured down the lower half of the wall. A red line surrounded the Altar at mid-height to separate the upper from the lower half. This line was located 1 cubit below the top of the middle platform, the Sovayv (Rambam, Bais HaB'chirah 2:9). To further emphasize this border, there was a floral design above the red line (Tiferes Yisroel).

To the south of the Altar was a ramp (Midos 3:3). Its slope was 32 cubits long, 16 cubits wide, and it was as tall as the Place of the Arrangement. There was a small gap between the ramp and the Altar (Rashi, Succah 49a). Some authorities say that the gap was 2 cubits (Chassam Sofer, Tamid 28b). Whenever new wood was brought to the top of the Altar, salt was sprinkled on the ramp to prevent slipping. At other times salt was not permitted because it would cause a separation between the feet of the priest and the Altar. During a service, there could be no intervening substance between the soles of the feet and the floor of the Temple. Even the wearing of shoes or stockings was not permitted. Carrying wood to the top of the Altar, however, was not considered a service (Eruvin 104a).

There were also two smaller side ramps (Zevachim 62b). One, to the east of the main ramp, led to the top of the Sovayv. The other was to the west of the main ramp and led to the top of the Foundation (Rashi, Zevachim 62b). These smaller ramps were 30 cubits long and 7 ⅚ cubits wide (Tavnis Haichel). All the ramps had small walls built along the sides to prevent the priests from falling off (Tiferes Yisroel).

There was a cubicle in which to place a slaughtered bird that was found to be unfit. External blemishes do not disqualify fowl; however, internal disorders and injuries do (treifah). If, after the bird was slaughtered, it was found to be unfit, it was discarded and tossed into this cubicle. Some sources say the cubicle was located on the western side of the main ramp, near the top (Rambam, Bais HaB'chirah 2:14). Others say it was a shallow pit located in the space between the ramp and the Altar, toward the west (Rashi, Pesachim 34a). Still others maintain that it was located on top of the ramp, at the upper end toward the west (Tiferes Yisroel).

23

The Dome of the Rock
and the Shis

On the top of the southwestern corner of the Foundation, two drains were carved. One was a little to the south, called the Southern Foundation, the other, slightly to the west, was called the Western Foundation (Midos 3:2). After the sacrificial service was performed with the blood, by pouring it against either the upper or the lower portion of the Altar's side, the remaining blood was poured onto the top of the Foundation. Two grooves were carved on top of the Foundation, which carried the blood into the drains (Tiferes Yisroel).

The blood from both drains mixed together in a channel and flowed out into the Kidron Valley, enriching the soil (Midos 3:2). The earth was sold to gardeners for fertilizer, and the monies brought in from the sale of the blood went to the Temple treasury (Rashi, Pesachim 22a).

There are various opinions as to the nature of the channel. Some say it was a brook that flowed through the courtyard of the Temple (Rav). Others say the channel had no water, but was merely a conduit to carry away the blood (Piskei Tosfos). Another opinion says that the channel was a sewer under the Altar (Rambam, Bais HaB'chirah 2:12). All opinions, however, agree that there was water flowing across the courtyard. They merely disagree as to whether the water can be identified as the channel of the Altar. Whenever the priests wanted to clean the floor of the courtyard, they blocked up the top of the sewer, causing the courtyard to flood. This would dissolve the dust. The sewer was then reopened, and the water would carry the dust into the valley below (Rashi, Pesachim 64a; Tavnis Haichel).

All opinions also recognize the existence of a sewer near the Altar. The sewer was directly connected to the two basins atop the Altar that were used on Succos for the Water and Wine Pouring ceremonies. Opinions differ as to whether that sewer was also connected to the two blood-drains on top of the Altar foundation.

The sewer located beneath the Altar was called the Shis (Plate 76, #41). The cover to the Shis was a marble tile 1 cubit by 1 cubit. It had a hoop set into it by which the tile could be raised (Midos 3:3). The Shis was a natural formation made during the Six Days of Creation. In fact, the first word of the Torah, "b'rayshis," "in the beginning," can also be read "barah shis," "He created the Shis" (Succah 49a).

When King David conquered Jerusalem, he found that the Shis was filled with earth, so he had it cleared out (Rashi, Succah 53a). Once every seventy years, young priests would go down into the Shis to clean it (Rashi, Succah 53a). Some authorities say that the jug of pure oil that the Maccabees found when they regained the Temple had been hidden in the Shis (Ezras Cohanim).

We stated earlier that the Altar rested on the ground itself, not on an elevated floor. This means that the ground level, or bedrock, must have been high at that point. We now also know that under the Altar was a sewer, a channel, that flowed out into the Kidron Valley. Let us see if we can locate the Shis.

Today, defiantly crowning the top of the Temple Mount is the Dome of the Rock. When it was first built and by whom is shrouded in mystery. The building is octagonal. This is not a Muslim style of architecture; it is Byzantine. Why would the Byzantines build on top of the Temple Mount? They were Christians, and the Christians placed no particular sanctity on the Temple Mount.

In 70 c.e., Titus burned the Holy Temple; however, because much of the structure was stone, the ruins of the Temple were still recognizable. In 135 c.e. Emperor Hadrian rebuilt the ruins into a pagan temple. The "ruins" of the Jewish Temple could still be seen. The rabbis of that time required that special prayers be recited by "one who views the ruins" and that the viewer rend his garments as a sign of mourning (Moed Katan 26a). In 320 c.e., under Constantine the Great, the Roman Empire became Christian and the seat of empire was moved to Byzantium. Constantine had no use for any temple, Jewish or pagan, atop the Mount, so he had it razed to its very foundations. Maps of that era show a bare Temple Mount.

In 623 C.E. the Persians invaded and captured Jerusalem from the Byzantines. It was through the assistance of the Jews who lived in Jerusalem, and who had suffered greatly at the hands of the Byzantines, that the Persians were victorious. In recognition of their help, the Persians passed many laws in favor of the Jews and prejudicial toward the Byzantine Christians. The Jews optimistically thought that the time of redemption was at hand, and began preparing for the rebuilding of the Temple. But the Jewish dream was dispelled. Within a short time, the Byzantines regained Jerusalem. In retaliation against the Jews, the Byzantines passed laws forbidding Jews to be in the vicinity of the Temple Mount. The Byzantines decided to build a church on top of the mountain to infuriate the Jews, and further dash their hopes of redemption.

By 638 C.E., Jerusalem had fallen into Muslim hands. The church was converted into a Muslim shrine, the Dome of the Rock. Muslims believed it marked the spot from which Muhammad ascended to heaven. Muslim sources confuse the issue because some credit the builder of the shrine as Abd al Malik of the Omayyad dynasty (685–705), while others credit Al Mamoun of the Abbassid dynasty (813–833). This can be attributed to interdenominational rivalry. In any event, the shrine is built around a rock. Tradition has always maintained that this rock was the Even Sh'siyah, the Foundation Stone of the Temple, the rock upon which the Holy Ark rested during the First Temple era, the site of the Holy of Holies (Plate 84) (Yoma 5:2).

The rock itself is 41 feet wide and 58 feet long and projects 6 feet above the shrine's floor. According to tradition and the Midrash, this was the site of the binding of Isaac by Abraham. Here Jacob dreamed of a ladder that reached the heavens, with angels ascending and descending (Pirkei D'Rebbi Eliezer, chap. 35). From this place God took the stone upon which He carved the first tablets (Zohar Parshas Yisro). From this very spot creation began (Yoma 54b).

On the southeastern portion of the Rock is an opening leading to a cave below (Plate 85) that the Muslims call the Well of Souls. The roof of the cave is seven feet below the top surface of the Rock. Fourteen steps lead eleven feet down to the cave, which is 9 feet high and 18 ½ feet long.

In 1865, Captain Charles Wilson was sent with the sanction of the British War Department to survey the water supply of Jerusalem. Many important archeological observations and discoveries

Plate 84. The Rock. The Dome of the Rock was built to enshrine this sacred rock. Note the cave entrance in the lower center.

Plate 85. The Cave. This accurate drawing was made during the Parker Expedition at the beginning of the twentieth century.

were made during his mission. When he returned to England, he wrote an account of his journey. His book, *Ordnance Survey of Jerusalem*, contains a preface by the director of the survey, Colonel Sir Henry James. Colonel James writes, "Beneath the Sakhra [Arabic for rock] there is a cave, which is entered by descending some steps on the south east side. A hole has been cut through from the upper surface of the rock into the chamber beneath, and there is a corresponding hole immediately under it, which leads to a drain down to the valley of the Kedron [sic]."

We now discover, to our amazement, that there is a drain in the floor of the cave that leads to the Kidron Valley. Could this be the Shis? Could the Rock be the place upon which the Altar stood? The Altar did rest on solid bedrock and not on an elevated platform. The mountain's bedrock must have been high at the point of the Altar. Could this be that point?

If this is so, then the Holy of Holies was located farther westward. The center of the Holy of Holies was about 103 cubits west of the Shis (Midos 3:6, 4:7). A cubit is between 18 and 24 inches. If our calculations and speculations are correct, then the Holy of Holies was between 154–206 feet west of the cave in the Rock. That would place the site of the Holy of Holies near the western steps leading up to the Dome of the Rock platform (Plate 86).

In the floor of the cave is a large, round, marble slab. It is said that this slab covers the entrance to another cave below. Legend says that anyone who enters that cavern never returns. Rabbi Dovid ben Zimra (Radvaz), who lived in Jerusalem in the 1500s, reports that ancient rulers would send men to their deaths by casting them into that cave (Radvaz, Shailos U'Tishuvos).

In 1911, a group of British adventurers known as the Parker Mission explored the cave. They found that the plastered walls and floor gave off a hollow sound when tapped. Rumor spread that they had found the Holy Ark, the Urim V'Tumim, and other Temple treasures. The rumors were, of course, not true.

Rabbi David Kimchi, who lived in France during the thirteenth century, well after the Dome of the Rock had been built, said that no one will ever build over the site of the Holy of Holies (Radak, Yeshaiyah 64:10). If the Holy of Holies was in fact located on the steps, then no nation has ever built over the site.

Earlier we found two tunnels in the vicinity of the Dome (see Plate 36). They started from a common point in the north, and one led straight in the direction of the Rock while the other veered toward the west. We can now speculate that the tunnel going toward the Rock was the tunnel of the Hearth, which was located opposite the Altar (Tiferes Yisroel and Ritvah, Yoma 15b). (In Maimonides' diagram, the Hearth is located opposite the Heichel; however, the eighteenth-century scholar Rabbi Yaakov Emden wrote that whoever drew the diagram erred.) The tunnel going north–south connected the Hearth with the priest's mikva. The tunnel veering to the west is the tunnel the Talmud refers to that went under the Heichel (Pesachim 86a).

This area has not been explored for over 100 years. The Muslims are most reluctant to allow any type of exploration and investigation of the Temple Mount. The imagination can only guess at what is still hidden at the ends of the tunnels. Perhaps the priest's mikva is still there. Alas, for now one can only wonder.

Plate 86. The western steps that led up to the Dome of the Rock. It is the author's contention that the Holy of Holies was located near the top of these steps.

24

The Butchering Place

North of the Altar was the Butchering Place where the sacrificial animals were slaughtered and butchered. In the northern section of the Butchering Place were eight small columns (Plate 76, #37). Resting on the columns were blocks of cedar wood, each of which had nine hooks set into it (Midos 3:5). The slaughtered carcass of the sacrificial animal was hung on these hooks in order to remove the skin and butcher the animal (Tiferes Yisroel). One block of wood was set onto each column (Tavnis Haichel). Some say that each block of wood was stretched across and supported by two columns. Therefore, there were eight columns but only four blocks of wood (Mileches Shlomo).

Three hooks were set into the northern side of the wood, three on the eastern side, and three on the southern side. There were no hooks on the western side, so that the priest did not have to turn his back to the Holy of Holies as he was butchering the animal. The hooks were three fists (t'fachim) long. One fist was set into the wood; two fists projected outward (Piskei Tosfos).

Nearby were eight tables (Plate 76, #38) (Midos 5:2; Rambam, Bais HaB'chirah 5:12) that served several purposes. The meat was washed on these tables before it was cooked and eaten by the priests (Rambam). The animal parts offered atop the Altar also had to be washed (Rav). The tables kept the carcass from touching the ground as it was being butchered (Tosfos, Yoma 16b). These tables could fold so they could be moved around as needed (R'shash,

Midos 5). According to some sources, there were separate tables for butchering and washing (Tosfos, Yoma 16b).

North of the Altar were twenty-four hoops (Plate 76, #39) set into the ground (Midos 3:5). There is a debate in the Talmud about the arrangement of the hoops. There were either six rows of four hoops each, or four rows of six each. In order to distract the animal before it was slaughtered, during the earlier years of the Second Temple, the priest would make a slit in the animal's forehead. The painless incision caused blood to flow, distracting the animal. The High Priest Yochanan abolished the practice, lest it might be thought that the slit constituted a blemish, and the Temple was offering blemished animals. He decreed that hoops be set into the ground, and the animal's head be inserted to keep it steady (Sotah 48a).

One commentator envisioned these hoops as small hooks set into the ground. A rope was tied around the animal's head, and the other end of the rope was passed through the hook. The rope was pulled until the animal's head was held securely near the ground (Aruch).

Another commentator had a completely different view of the hoops. There were twenty-four rings, or hoops, set into the ground before the Altar. There were also twenty-four priestly groups. Each group served one week, each group had a name, and the name of each group was carved into the hoop. When a new priestly group began its week, they would remove the hoop with their name on it and set it against the wall near the end of the butchering area so that all could know the name of the group that was serving (Rambam, Mishnayos Succah, end).

25

Between the Altar
and the Heichel

The end of the Altar to the front wall of the Heichel measured 22 cubits (Midos 3:6). In that area toward the south was the washbasin (Plate 76, #42). Every priest had to wash his hands and feet before performing the day's Temple service. We have very little in the way of a description of the basin. Its upper rim had a circumference of 12 cubits (Tosfos Yom Tov) and originally had only two faucets. Ben Katin, a High Priest (Rashi, Yoma 37a), added another ten faucets (Yoma 37a). It is not known whether the twelve faucets formed a spiral going around the basin, or if one faucet was above and the other eleven were in a straight line below (Meleches Shlomo).

The basin was a holy vessel. Any water or other liquid that was left overnight in a holy vessel was unfit for use the following day. In the Temple each morning the priests had to refill the basin. It was a tedious task. Ben Katin had a mechanism consisting of levers and pulleys that lifted the basin and lowered it into a pit of water, where it remained overnight. The pit was not considered a vessel, so the waters would not become unfit for use. Some say that it was not a pit that was dug near the basin, but rather a large vessel of water, which was not proclaimed sacred, that was used for this purpose (Rambam, quoted by Rav).

The next morning the basin was raised and set into place. The first sound heard in the Temple every morning was the sound of

Ben Katin's device raising the basin (Tamid 1:4), a sound that could be heard as far away as Jericho (Tamid 3:8).

Earlier we discussed two complexes of buildings. The first consisted of the Supreme Court Chamber, the Chamber of the High Priest, and the Chamber of the Well (Plate 76, #18, #19, #20). The second complex comprised the Salt Room, Parvah's Chamber, and the Chamber of the Rinsers (Plate 76, #21, #22, #23). We know that these two complexes were on opposite sides of the Temple courtyard, one in the north and the other in the south. However, in various texts, there are differences of opinion about which was where. Based on practicality and some circumstantial evidence, it may be said that the Salt Room complex was in the north, and the Supreme Court Chamber in the south.

To the north of the Altar was the Butchering Place. There, the carcasses were skinned and flayed, so it makes sense that the tannery, Parvah's Chamber, would be nearby. Here was where the animals' internal organs were removed, so it also makes sense that the Chamber of the Rinsers would be nearby. And because the meat was washed and salted here, too, it seems logical to assume that the Salt Chamber would be nearby. (Salt was also used in the preservation of leather.)

The High Priest's Chamber was part of the Supreme Court complex. Another name for this room was the Wood Chamber. On the southern wall of the Azarah was a gateway through which firewood was carried. It would have made sense to have a room nearby in which to store the wood, because even though there was a Chamber of the Wood in the Women's Courtyard, that was where the wood was sorted.

Another room in the Supreme Court complex was the Chamber of the Well. Some say that the mechanism that Ben Katin had constructed lowered the basin into the well in the Chamber of the Well (Ravyah), so obviously, the Chamber of the Well had to be located in the south near the basin.

Twelve steps (Plate 76, #43) led from the end of the Altar to the entranceway of the Heichel. Each step was half a cubit high. The depth of the steps varied. The bottom step was 1 cubit deep, the second step 1 cubit deep, and the third 3 cubits deep. The sequence was as follows, starting with the bottom step: 1, 1, 3, 1, 1, 3,   1, 1, 3,   1, 1, 4 (some say 5) (Midos 3:6). According to one text, all twelve steps were half a cubit deep (Rambam, Bais HaB'chirah 6:4).

As there were twelve steps leading to the entrance of the

Heichel, and each step was half a cubit high, the floor of the Heichel must have been 6 cubits higher than the floor of the Courtyard of the Priests.

Four steps led up from the Courtyard of the Israelites into the Courtyard of the Priests. The bottom step was 1 cubit high; the other three steps were half a cubit high. Thus, the Courtyard of the Priests was 2½ cubits higher than the Courtyard of the Israelites.

Fifteen steps led from the Women's Courtyard into the Courtyard of the Israelites. Each step was half a cubit high. Therefore, the Courtyard of the Israelites must have been 7½ cubits higher than the Women's Courtyard.

Twelve steps led into the Women's Courtyard. Each of those steps was half a cubit high; therefore, the Women's Courtyard must have been 6 cubits higher than the outer floor of the Temple Mount. We can conclude that the floor of the Heichel was 22 cubits higher than the floor of the outer yard.

26

The Hall

The largest and most ornate complex in the Temple was the Heichel (Plate 76, #45, 47, 48). Yosiphon describes what he saw:

> The stones with which the king [Herod] built the Sanctuary were white as snow. A single stone was twenty-five cubits in length, twelve cubits in width, and eight cubits high, marble stones. Each stone was identical, from the foundations until the top of the building. The sanctuary rose up very high. It could be seen from anywhere in the city and from afar.
>
> The doors were fashioned most ornately. The doorposts, lintels, the knobs, and hinges were all made of silver. Over each door hung a curtain the same size as the door. Woven curtains, made of gold, blue wool, purple wool, and scarlet threads, set with precious gems and points of gold and blue wool, most beautiful. Each curtain had a border of a golden floral design.
>
> There were pillars of gold with silver bases and golden hooks. He fashioned a sculpture of grape clusters and leaves and vines out of the purest gold and hung the sculpture atop the pillars. One thousand talents [approximately 2,400,000 ounces] of the purest gold was its weight. These clusters were fashioned with the greatest of wisdom. The tendrils, leaves, and blossoms were of sparkling gold; the clusters of greenish gold, and the berries of precious gems. All the work was intricate and detailed. It was a wonder to behold, and brought joy to all that saw it. Many in Rome testified to this, for they saw it in the house that they destroyed. [*Yosiphon*, chap. 55, p. 193]

This wonderous cluster of grapes hung in the great hall (Plate 87) that was the front of the Heichel. The doorway to the hall or portico was 20 cubits wide and 40 cubits high. It was the largest doorway in the Temple (Midos 3:7). The facade rose 100 cubits (Midos 4:6). Above the doorway were five great mahogany beams set into the face of the building (Midos 3:7), each carved with ornate designs (Rav). The bottom beam was set directly above the doorway and was 22 cubits long, extending beyond the doorway 1 cubit on each side. The second beam was 24 cubits long and positioned above the first beam, beyond which it extended 1 cubit on each side. So it was with the other beams up to the fifth beam, which was 30 cubits long. Set between the beams were rows of stones projecting from the wall (Midos 3:7).

The entrance had no doors, but rather a large curtain of the finest linen, with fringes, and flowers of gold embroidered on it (Tavnis Haichel). Worked into this curtain was a panorama of the universe. Scarlet thread denoted fire, fine linen the earth, blue wool the sky, and purple wool the oceans (Josephus, *The Jewish War*, Book 5, chap. 5, para. 4).

Flanking the entrance were two large copper columns. Each was 18 cubits high, 12 cubits in circumference, ⅔ of a cubit thick, and

Plate 87. The facade of the Heichel. Sources differ as to whether the engraving of the Menorah was on the facade of the hall or above the inner Heichel doorway.

had a capital on top, 5 cubits high, carved with flowers and lilies (Ezras Cohanim). The right column was called Yachin, representing the kingdom of David forever prepared (Yachin in Hebrew). The left column was called Boaz after the judicial ancestor of David (Rashi, 2 Chronicles 3:17). The medieval Jewish traveler, Benjamin of Tudela, reports seeing these two copper columns in Rome in the church of St. Stephen (Seder HaDoros).

There are various descriptions of what the Hall must have looked like. Some say that it had only three walls. There was no front wall. The width of the hall was 20 cubits, the size of the entrance or open front (Tosfos, Avodah Zorah 43a). Some imagine it the other way, with only a front wall and no side walls (Shita Mikubetzes, Menachos 28b). However, most authorities describe the Hall as 100 cubits long from north to south, 100 cubits high, and 11 cubits wide from east to west (Tiferes Yisroel). The walls were 5 cubits thick (Midos 4:7). It was one story high, and chains were suspended from the ceiling to the ground so that young priests could climb the chains to inspect the walls and windows for needed repairs (Rosh).

Beams of cedar connected the front and back walls and served as braces to keep the high walls from toppling (Midos 3:8). There were two large windows in front (Rosh; however, Tiferes Yisroel's diagram has six windows). They had arched tops and all kinds of decorative designs (Rosh). During the dedication ceremony of the Second Temple in the time of Ezra, crowns were placed on the heads of Yehoshua ben Yehotzadok, the High Priest, and Zerubavel, the leader of the Jews ("Nasi" or Prince as he was called during the Second Temple and post-Second Temple era). Later the crowns were placed above the windows (Tavnis Haichel).

Inside the Hall was a place for the High Priest to eat his portion of the sacrificial meat (Rashi, Ezekiel 44:23). Some say this place was designated for the king (Metzudos, Ezekiel 44:23).

The golden grapes that Yosiphon described earlier are mentioned in the Talmud. It further states that they once had to be moved, and three hundred priests were required for the task (Midos 3:8). However, that was merely hyperbole and is not to be taken literally (Chullin 90b).

At the northern and southern ends of the Hall were two rooms called the Chambers of the Knives (Plate 76, #46). Together these rooms measured 11 cubits from east to west, and 10 cubits from north to south, excluding the thickness of the walls (Midos 4:7). The slaughtering knives were kept here in cubicles set into the western wall (Rashi, Zevachim 54b). The dull or defective knives were kept in the southern room, where they were sharpened and repaired. The knives suitable for use were stored in the northern room (Tavnis Haichel).

Inside the Hall was the doorway leading into the first chamber, the Kodesh (Plate 76, #47). The name Heichel is sometimes used to denote the entire building, and sometimes it is used as a synonym for the Kodesh. Outside the doorway of the Kodesh, in the Hall, were two tables, one of marble, one of gold. The marble table to the right of the doorway was used to hold the twelve new showbreads that were to be set on the Golden Table (shulchan) that was inside the Heichel. Every Sabbath, the old loaves of showbread were removed, one by one, from the Golden Table. As each old showbread was removed, it was placed on the table fashioned from gold to the left of the doorway. A new showbread, taken from the marble table, was set in place of the bread that had been removed (Tavnis Haichel). On the Golden Table were two silver spoons filled with frankincense. During the Sabbath, the frankincense was offered on top of the Altar, after which the old showbread was divided among the priests and eaten.

In the southwest and northwest corners of the Hall were doors 8 cubits high. All sacrifices had to be slaughtered "opposite the door of the Tent of Assembly." In order to facilitate slaughtering in the southwestern and northwestern sections of the Azarah, these two doors were built so that slaughtering done anywhere in the Azarah would be "opposite the door" (Zevachim 55b).

The Rambam had a unique view of the Hall and of the entire Heichel. His opinion is presented in chapter 31.

27

The Kodesh

The doorway of the Kodesh (Plate 88) was 10 cubits wide and 20 cubits high (Midos 4:1). Over the doorway was a carving of a golden menorah donated by Queen Helena, a convert to Judaism. The morning service could not begin before sunrise. The Temple was surrounded by high walls, and it was not possible to see the rising sun, so priests had to be sent outside to see if it was time for the service to begin. After Queen Helena donated the menorah, it was no longer necessary to send a priest outside the Temple. As the sun rose in the east it shone against the menorah and the reflected light was cast into the Azarah. The priests then knew that the morning service could begin (Yoma 37a).

The doorway was 6 cubits thick and had four doors (Midos 4:1, 7). The doors were made of olive wood overlaid with gold. Carved in the gold were angels, palm trees, and flowers (1 Kings 6:32; Tavnis Haichel). The front walls of the Heichel and the doorposts were 6 cubits thick. Two doors were set at the front of the 6-cubit-thick doorway, and two doors were set at the rear. The front two doors opened inward, and folded against the inner wall of the doorway. The rear doors also opened inward, and folded against the wall (Plate 89). (Rebbe Yehudah has a different opinion concerning the doors [Plate 90] [Midos 4:1].) When the doors were opened in the morning, their creaking could be heard as far away as Jericho (Tamid 30a).

In front of the doors was a curtain that could be raised and

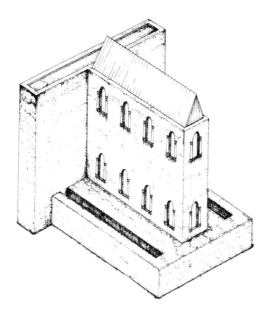

Plate 88. The Heichel seen from the northwest.

lowered (Yoma 54a). When the High Priest was in the Kodesh, the curtain was lowered to afford him privacy (Tiferes Yisroel, Tamid 7:1).

The windows of the Kodesh were 20 cubits high, and consisted of long narrow openings in the walls. The openings were wider on the outside than on the inside (Tavnis Haichel). In a private dwelling, window openings were narrow on the outside and wide on the inside to cause the light to spread inside. The rabbis viewed the Heichel as the "light source" of the world, so the windows were constructed thus to spread the light outward. The Kodesh was 40 cubits long, 20 cubits wide and 40 cubits high (Midos 4:6–7). The walls were paneled with wood and overlaid with gold, except

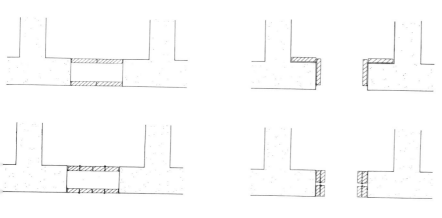

Plate 89. The four doors that form the entrance of the Kodesh in closed position and open position.

Plate 90. Rebbe Yehudah's eight doors that form the entrance of the Kodesh in closed and open positions.

The Kodesh **125**

for the places the doors covered when they were open (Midos 4:1). Engraved in the gold were palm trees, vines, flowers, and angels (Yoma 54b; Rashi, 1 Kings 6:29). The ceiling contained deeply carved decorative work 1 cubit thick; the entire ceiling was 5 cubits thick. The first cubit was the decorative carving, and above this were 2 cubits of thick boards. Some sources say that in this 2-cubit space was a cistern that contained the rainwater that flowed off the roof. Another cistern was built into the ceiling of the room above the Kodesh. The rainwater would first flow into the upper cistern, and the overflow would run off through pipes into the lower cistern. Along the southern side of the Heichel was a large pool surrounded by walls where the water eventually accumulated (Rambam, Bais HaB'chirah 4).

Above the 2-cubit space in the ceiling was 1 cubit of narrow boards, and atop it was 1 cubit of thick plaster, which also served as the floor for the room above (Midos 4:6).

On the golden floor of the Kodesh was a tile that could be lifted by a ring that was set into it. When it was lifted, earth could be seen below. The earth for the bitter waters of the unfaithful wife was taken from here (Sotah 2:2).

The entire Heichel rested upon a foundation 6 cubits high, which implies that the floor of the Kodesh was 6 cubits above ground level. How did they get the earth for the bitter waters if ground level was so far below? The opening in the floor was 1 cubit by 1 cubit; perhaps a priest was lowered through the opening to bring up the earth. Another possibility is that the mountain sloped upward at this point, bringing the ground level up to the floor level of the Kodesh.

Near the northern wall of the Kodesh was the Golden Table (Plate 91). It was placed in an east–west orientation (Menachos 88a). On the Table were the twelve showbreads and two spoons filled with frankincense. There were ten other golden tables in the Kodesh; five north of the Golden Table, and five to the south. These were to enhance the beauty of the Golden Table itself (Yoma 51b).

The Menorah was placed with a north–south orientation near the southern wall of the Kodesh (Plate 92) (Rambam, Bais HaB'chirah 3), though some say it was placed with an east–west orientation (Raavad). There were ten other menorahs in the Kodesh. Five were placed north of the Menorah, and five were placed to the south. These, too, were for ornamental purposes (Menachos 99a).

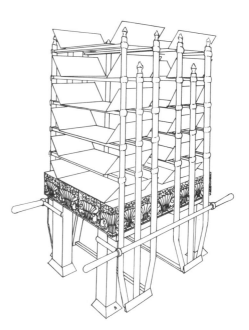

Plate 91. The Golden Table. The Twelve Showbreads, representing the Tribes of Israel, rested on the shelves of the Table.

Plate 92. A stained glass representation of the Menorah. The window is in the Heichel Shlomo Synagogue.

In the center of the Kodesh was the Golden Altar (Plate 93). The Menorah, Altar, and Table were placed within the inner half of the Kodesh (Tosefta, Yoma 2; however, Rambam, Bais HaB'chirah 3 says within the inner third). The Altar was slightly off to the east.

In the First Temple, a wall 1 cubit thick separated the Kodesh from the Holy of Holies (Plate 76, #48). In that Temple the ceiling was only 30 cubits above the floor, and a one-cubit-thick wall could be erected to a height of 30 cubits. The Second Temple had a height of 40 cubits between floor and ceiling. A wall 1 cubit thick could not be erected to the 40 cubit height. They did not want to make a wider wall so as not to diminish any area of the Kodesh or the Holy of Holies. It was decided that a curtain would be used. The rabbis were not certain if the wall that separated the Kodesh from the Holy of Holies in the First Temple was located within the 40-cubit length of the Kodesh or within the 20-cubit length of the Holy of Holies. Therefore, it was decided to build the Kodesh a full 40 cubits long and the Holy of Holies a full 20 cubits. A neutral space of 1 cubit would be placed between them, and marked off by two curtains. One curtain was placed between the end of the Kodesh and the beginning of the cubit space. The other curtain was placed between the end of the cubit space and the beginning of the Holy of Holies. The outer curtain was folded back on its southern side and the inner curtain folded back on its northern side (Yoma 51b, 52b).

The 1-cubit space was called the traksin cubit, which may be a

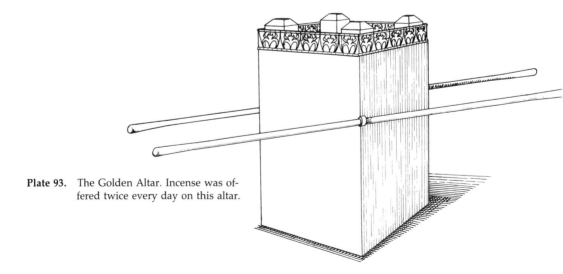

Plate 93.   The Golden Altar. Incense was offered twice every day on this altar.

contraction of the Aramaic "tarak sin," the Wall of Sinai, Sinai referring to the Ark and the tablets. It may be derived from the Greek trac-syn (in-out) which may have meant that they were not certain if the area was within the Kodesh or outside (Tosfos, Yoma 51b). In the Second Temple there was neither a wall nor any Sinaic tablet or Ark, so if traksin means the Sinai Wall, possibly the term originated in First Temple times, referring to the wall that separated the Kodesh from the Holy of Holies, and was carried over into the Second Temple era. There is an opinion that the Ark, together with the tablets, was hidden under the Holy of Holies (Yoma 53b) (Tiferes Yisroel, Midos 4:7).

The curtains were never opened except during festivals, when they were rolled back so that the people could see the carvings of the angels on the wall. The angels in the carvings were embracing, which represented the love of God for the children of Israel (Yoma 54a).

28

The Menorah

With the downfall of Judea in 70 C.E., the Menorah became the national symbol of the Jewish people. The victorious Roman general, Titus, son of Emperor Vespasian, had an arch of triumph erected in Rome. The arch was completed by his son Domitian after Titus's death (Plate 94). Depicted on the walls of the arch were Roman soldiers carrying off the Menorah from the destroyed Temple of the Jews (Plate 95). It was the Romans' depiction of the vanquished Menorah that came to symbolize the hopes and prayers, the degradation and the tragedy of the wandering Jews.

A triumphal parade was held in Rome to commemorate the victory over Judea. Josephus described the events as he saw them.

> While it was still night all the soldiers marched out under their commanders to the temple of Isis, for the generals had slept there that night. At daybreak, Vespasian and Titus came out, wreathed in laurels and wearing the traditional purple robes. A dais had been set up before the facade of the temple and ivory chairs were placed for them. As they sat the troops cheered. Vespasian acknowledged the cheers, and the troops burst forth more loudly than before. The emperor gave the signal for silence. The crowd was hushed. Vespasian arose and recited the customary prayer. After a short speech, the emperor dismissed the troops for a morning feast.
>
> Great movable stages passed by the celebrants. Some were three and four stories high. Tapestries interwoven with gold and frames of gold and ivory hung from the stages. The war

Plate 94. The Arch of Titus. Built by Titus's son, Domitian, its inner walls depict the Menorah and the downfall of Judea.

Plate 95. A closeup of the Menorah depicted in the Arch of Titus. Note the double hexagon base.

and all its battles were portrayed on these stages. On one stage, Roman soldiers stood proudly brandishing their swords. On another, the enemy in flight. And on yet another, the victors leading the captives off to Rome. Stages with great walls and enemy defenders on top, with battle engines mercilessly pounding at the walls, and great torrents of blood flowing down. Stages with temples and houses set ablaze

The Menorah **131**

rolled down the procession way on great movable stages. On each stage stood a commander in a pose of victory. Stages with boats and ships heaped with the spoils of war, piled up indiscriminately. The more prominent treasures were carried high by the troops. They consisted of a golden table weighing many talents and a menorah also made of gold. After these, and the last of all the spoils, was a Torah, the scroll of Jewish Law. Then came a group carrying images of victory, all fashioned of gold and ivory. Then came Vespasian, and then Titus with his son, Domitian, at his side, mounted on a decorated horse that was a sight unto itself.

The triumphal procession concluded at the temple of Jupiter Capitoline. Simon ben Gorius, the general of the Jewish zealots, who had been marching in the procession among the prisoners, was brought forth. Before the eyes of the jubilant crowd, Simon was duly executed.

When the ceremonies had concluded, Vespasian ordered the erection of a Temple of Peace. In a short time it was completed and its style surpassed all comprehension. In it he placed the golden vessels of the Temple, for he took great pride in them. But the Torah scroll and the purple curtain which hung in the sanctuary he took to his palace for safe keeping. [Josephus, *The Jewish War*, Book 7, chap. 5]

So wrote Josephus, who saw the procession in Rome and recorded those events for all time. We can picture the jubilation of the Romans' celebration of the downfall of Judea, an insignificant territory with no natural resources worth having, but with a belief and spirit worth defending. The conquest of Judea took longer than any other Roman conquest and many of the common folk believed that Judea must have been a mighty empire. And so the Romans rejoiced greatly when they saw the treasures of the fallen nation.

What has happened to these sacred objects? Many stories are told. One relates that the treasures were later taken to Byzantium and remained there until 1204, when they disappeared during the Fourth Crusade.

Were these captured spoils the actual Menorah and Golden Table from the Temple? Two points are worth noting. First, Josephus did not refer to the Golden Table and the Menorah as *the* Golden Table and *the* Menorah, but simply as *a* golden table and *a* menorah. There were many golden tables in the Temple, and many menorahs. Only one table contained the showbread and only one menorah was lit by the priest each day in the Kodesh.

Second, the menorah depicted on the arch of triumph has a

double hexagon for a base. On each side of each hexagon is a representation of each of the twelve tribes of Israel. Traditionally, the Menorah has always been pictured with a three-footed base (Rashi, Exodus, 25:31; Tosfos ad loc.). In Maimonides' halachic compendium, he says that the three-footed base was required by traditional law (Rambam, Bais HaB'chirah 3:2). Throughout history, the base of the Menorah has been depicted with three legs. Even an engraving made in Jerusalem while the Temple still stood shows a three-footed base (Plate 96). It would appear, therefore, that the Romans did not carry off *the* Menorah but rather one of the many other candelabra that stood in the Temple.

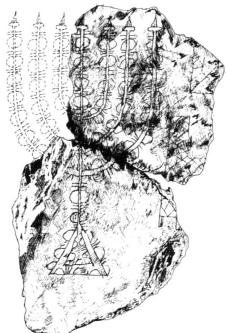

Plate 96. An engraving of the Menorah made while the Second Temple was still standing.

29

The Holy of Holies

The Holy of Holies, as its name implies, was the most sacred part of the entire Temple. Entry was forbidden except on Yom Kippur when the High Priest entered the inner sanctuary.

Its dimensions were 20 cubits long, 20 cubits wide, and 40 cubits high (Midos 4:6–7). The floor, walls, and ceiling were plated with gold, as was the Kodesh. However, the gold decorations in the Kodesh were carved into the wall, and in the Holy of Holies they were embossed (Abarbanel, 1 Kings 6:27).

In the Holy of Holies was a rock that projected above the ground to a height of 3 fingers (Yoma 5:2). The rock was first uncovered by King David and the prophet Samuel (Sota 48b). Some say the rock was in the very center of the Holy of Holies (Tosfos Yom Tov); others say it was near the western wall of the Holy of Holies (Rambam, Bais HaB'chirah 4), and still others maintain that it was near the curtains separating the Kodesh and the Holy of Holies (Tosfos, Baba Basra 25a).

The Ark rested upon the rock during the First Temple era. During the Second Temple there was no Ark. Some say it was captured by Nebuchadnezzar; others say it was hidden beneath the rock; and still others say that it was hidden below the Wood Chamber in the Women's Courtyard (Plate 97) (Yoma 52b).

There was another floor level above the Kodesh and Holy of Holies whose dimensions and decorative work were exactly like the chambers below, but with no curtains separating the floor

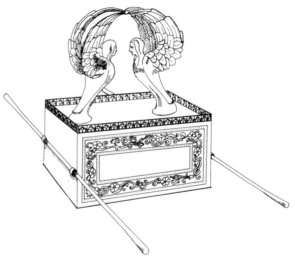

Plate 97. The Holy Ark. The Ark was hidden by the Prophet Jeremiah toward the end of the First Temple era and has never been rediscovered. In the Second Temple the Holy of Holies was bare. Page 146 discusses the possible location of this sacred treasure.

above the Kodesh from the floor above the Holy of Holies. Instead, stone blocks projected from the wall itself to mark the division between the two sacred areas (Midos 4:5).

The floor of the chamber above the Holy of Holies had trapdoors surrounding the walls of the room. A large box, supported by a rope, could be lowered through any trapdoor down into the Holy of Holies. Workers who had to repair the walls of the Holy of Holies were lowered through the trapdoors into the chamber below. Their view of the Holy of Holies was completely blocked off except for the portion of the wall to be repaired (Midos 4:5).

According to halacha, workmen were actually permitted to enter the Holy of Holies directly. However, the rabbis decided to make the rules more stringent, so that the workmen could not feast their eyes upon the sacred room. Thus the system of trapdoors and the large wooden box was instituted (Pesachim 26a).

The outer walls of the entire Heichel were 100 cubits high, and the roof rose up another 20 cubits (*Yosiphon*, chap. 55). The roof was sloped until it came to a 1-cubit flat surface on top, similar to Noah's ark (Rashi, Moed Katan 9a).

Surrounding the edge of the roof on top was a stone wall either 3 or 4 cubits high (Midos 4:6). To discourage birds from sitting on the wall of the Heichel and defiling it, a device called a raven-ender was installed (Midos 4:6). Some say this was a group of spikes 1 cubit long (Rosh). Others say it was a thin sheet of metal with a blade-like upper edge (Rav). Still others say it was a small metal scarecrow 1 cubit high (Aruch). Another opinion says that surrounding the top of the wall was a sheet of metal with a blade-like upper edge, and on top of the roof, where it narrowed to a 1-cubit width, were spikes (Rashi, Moed Katan 9a; Rashi, Shabbos 90a).

The Holy of Holies 135

30

Small Offices

Along the northern, western, and southern outside walls of the Kodesh and Holy of Holies were a series of small offices (Plate 98). The offices were three stories high. There were fifteen offices to the north, five per floor. Likewise there were fifteen small offices to the south. There were eight small offices to the west, three at the bottom level, three atop them, and two atop them (Plate 76, #50) (Midos 4:4).

The length and height of the offices are not recorded. However, since the Kodesh and Holy of Holies, including the traksin cubit, had a total length of 61 cubits, and along the northern side, for example, were five offices at the bottom level, the length of each office, including the thickness of the walls, was about 12⅕ cubits. The length of the western wall of the Holy of Holies was 20 cubits, and behind it, at the lowest level, were three offices. Each office was about 6⅔ cubits long. The three stories of offices had a total height of approximately 20 cubits. (Tavnis Haichel says 15 to 25 cubits.) The height of the Kodesh and Holy of Holies was 40 cubits. The offices covered the first 20 cubits of height of the outside wall of the Kodesh and Holy of Holies. The remaining 20 cubits had windows set into the walls to allow light to enter. The windows were 20 cubits high (Tavnis Haichel). Some say the offices attained a height equal to that of the Kodesh and Holy of Holies, which was 40 cubits (Raavad). According to this opinion, the offices must have

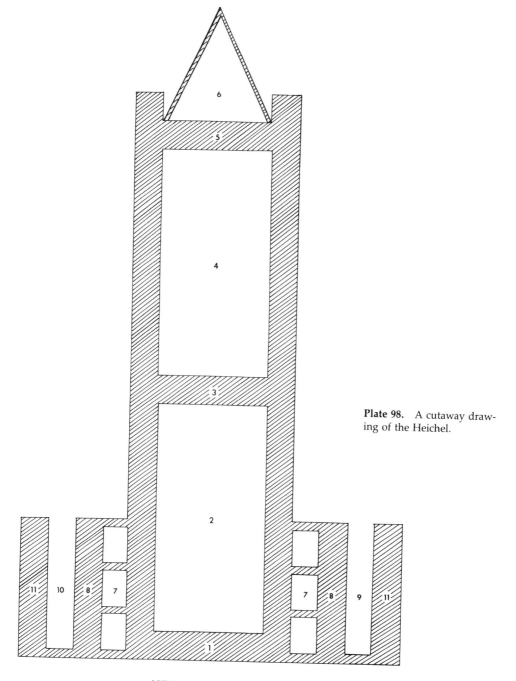

Plate 98. A cutaway drawing of the Heichel.

KEY TO PLATE 98

1– foundation
2– Kodesh
3– ceiling above Kodesh
4– upper story of Kodesh
5– ceiling above upper story
6– roof

7– small offices
8– back wall of offices
9– ramp
10– cistern
11– outer Heichel wall

had windows on the outside and inside walls to allow the light to pass from the outside into the Kodesh.

The Holy of Holies had one window in the back wall, 8 cubits high (Zevachim 55b).

The width of the offices is recorded. The bottom offices were only 5 cubits wide, the middle floor of offices 6 cubits wide, and the top floor of offices 7 cubits wide. The thickness of the walls of the Kodesh and Holy of Holies varied according to the width of the adjacent offices. The walls at the bottom were thicker, thus allowing an office to be only 5 cubits wide. The walls farther up were narrower, allowing for an office 7 cubits wide (Midos 4:4). The floor of the Kodesh and Holy of Holies was built on a foundation 6 cubits high. The bottom level of offices was built alongside the foundation, not above it (Tiferes Yisroel). Steps in each office led to the floor above and the floor below. Doors led into the adjacent offices, and steps were built inside the wall (Tavnis Haichel).

In the Hall doors led into the first office along the northern wall and into the first office along the southern wall (Plate 76 #49). The door leading to the first southern office was never opened by any priest. Concerning this door the prophet Ezekiel said, "And God told unto me, 'This door should be closed, not opened. Man shall not passed through it, for this is the entrance of the Lord, the God of Israel, though it be closed'" (Ezekiel 45) (Midos 4:2). However, on the Sabbath, festivals, and at the moment the new moon appeared, the door would open by itself (Pirkei D'Rebbe Eliezer 51).

Since the first floor of offices was located at the foundation level, these two doors in the Hall must have led into the first office on the second level (Rambam, Bais HaB'chirah 4:11).

To allow a person to stand in the Hall and open the door leading into the first northern office, an opening was located in the lower part of the door. The priest or Levite had to bend down, insert his hand through the opening, and, with a key, unlock the door from the inside (Tiferes Yisroel, Tamid 3:6). Inside that office was another doorway leading into the Kodesh. That door unlocked in a more conventional manner (Tiferes Yisroel, Tamid 3:6; Rashi, Baba Metzia 33a). Once inside the Kodesh, the Kodesh doors could be unlocked. The locks to these doors were on the insides of the doors.

The first northern office also had a door in its northern wall, which led to the bottom of a ramp (Tiferes Yisroel, Midos 4:7). The ramp (Plate 76, #51) led up to the roof of the western offices. One could walk along that roof, headed south, until he came to the southern side of the Heichel. There was another ramp along the southern side of the Heichel, on the roof of the southern offices, that led to a door into the chamber above the Kodesh (Tiferes Yisroel). Some say it was not a ramp but a ladder or staircase that led from the southern office roof to the chamber above the Kodesh (Vilna Gaon). Only workmen who had to do repair work went into this upper chamber.

Behind the southern wall of the southern offices was a cistern (Plate 76, #53). The water that flowed off the roof of the Heichel ran into that cistern (Tiferes Yisroel, Midos 4:7).

31

Maimonides' Heichel

According to most commentaries, the Heichel was constructed as we have described in the preceding pages. The Mishna says that the total length of the Heichel was 100 cubits, and its total width 100 cubits. The commentaries picture a T-shaped building, with the top of the T 100 cubits and the neck 100 cubits.

Maimonides had a radically different view. He pictured the Heichel as a square building. The commentaries described the Chambers of the Knives as small extensions of the Hall; Maimonides said that the Chambers of the Knives were 100-cubit-long chambers running along the northern and southern sides of the Heichel. The commentaries described the outside walls of the Heichel as consisting of large smooth stones. Maimonides envisioned alternate layers of projecting stones. The bottom layer was flat. One cubit up was a series of stones that projected outward 1 cubit. One cubit above that was another smooth layer of stones, and above that layer was a series of stones that projected out 3 cubits. And so they alternated: smooth layer, series projecting out 1 cubit, smooth layer, series projecting out 3 cubits. The uppermost layer was a series that projected out 4 cubits. Maimonides' internal floor plan also differs radically from those of the other commentators. For a detailed diagram of Maimonides' Heichel, see Plates 99 and 100.

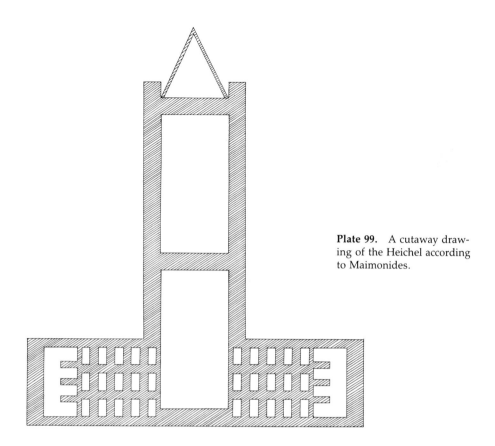

Plate 99. A cutaway drawing of the Heichel according to Maimonides.

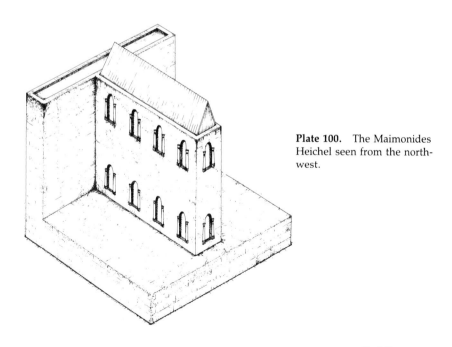

Plate 100. The Maimonides Heichel seen from the northwest.

32

Where Was
the Temple Located?

The question that haunts every student of the Holy Temple is, exactly where did the Holy Temple stand? For many years there was great uncertainty about the wall that surrounds the Temple Mount. The Western or Wailing Wall is part of the original Herodian wall, but what about the rest of the wall that surrounds the mountain? Is that, too, part of the original Herodian wall, or is it perhaps some later construction that has nothing to do with the original Temple?

We have already discussed the unique Herodian ashlars, with their recessed margins and smoothly polished centers. These magnificent stones can be traced around the entire wall that stands today. Some of the smaller ashlars that were knocked down have since been rebuilt higher up into more modern parts of the wall. But the enormous lower ashlars are still in place. Because they can be traced along all four walls, it is safe to assume that the Temple Compound enclosure we see today is that of Herod's time.

Herod's wall enclosed the Herodian extension to the Temple Mount. Somewhere inside stood the Holy Temple and its walls. If there were some way to determine the distance from the outer Herodian wall to the inner Temple walls, we would know the exact location of the Holy Temple. But, alas, no such measurements are known. We shall have to take a different approach.

The Dome of the Rock is a shrine built to protect the treasure within the rock. But what, exactly, is that rock? Legend tells us that this was the rock that was in the Holy of Holies (Radvaz); but, as I demonstrated earlier, there is a strong probability that this rock is near the spot upon which the Altar was built. Therefore, let us assume that there are two viable possibilities, that the rock is either the site of the Altar or the site of the Holy of Holies. What are the distances from these two points to the four walls of the Azarah? Based on figures from the Mishna in Midos, these distances can be calculated. First let us assume the rock to be the place of the Holy of Holies. The figures are as follows:

1. From the center of the Holy of Holies to the northern wall of the Azarah – 67½ cubits.

2. From the center of the Holy of Holies to the southern wall of the Azarah – 67½ cubits.

3. From the center of the Holy of Holies to the eastern wall of the Azarah (the Nicanor Gate) – 149 cubits.

4. From the center of the Holy of Holies to the western wall of the Azarah – 38 cubits.

The next step is to measure how far it was from the walls of the Azarah to the outside walls of the sacred Temple area. Unfortunately, neither the Mishna nor the Talmud records these measurements. Maimonides does not mention them either. The Shiltai HaGiborim does, however, give us the following distances.

A. From the northern wall of the Azarah to the northern wall of the Temple – 100 cubits.

B. From the southern wall of the Azarah to the southern wall of the Temple – 265 cubits.

C. From the eastern wall of the Azarah to the eastern wall of the Temple – 250 cubits.

D. From the western wall of the Azarah to the western wall of the Temple – 63 cubits.

It should be noted that the source for the Shiltai HaGiborim's figures are somewhat of a mystery. Nevertheless, according to the Shiltai HaGiborim the total distance from the center of the Holy of Holies to the northern wall of the Azarah was 167.5 cubits (Figure 1 plus Figure A). The total distance from the Holy of Holies to the southern wall of the Azarah was 332.5 cubits (Figure 2 plus Figure B). The total distance from the Holy of Holies to the eastern wall of the Azarah was 399 cubits (Figure 3 plus Figure C). The total distance from the Holy of Holies to the western wall of the Azarah was 101 cubits (Figure 4 plus Figure D).

The length and width of the Azarah was 500 cubits by 500 cubits. According to the Shiltai HaGiborim the length from the north to the Holy of Holies was 167.5 cubits. From the Holy of Holies to the south was 332.5 cubits—a total of 500 cubits. According to the Shiltai HaGiborim the distance from the eastern wall of the Azarah to the Holy of Holies was 399 cubits. From the Holy of Holies to the western wall was 101 cubits—a total length from east to west of 500 cubits.

The Chuldah Tunnels led from the southern Herodian wall underneath the southern Herodian extension into the sacred precincts of the Temple Mount. We can safely assume that the Southern Temple wall reached to the ends of the Chuldah Tunnels or at least close to them (Plate 101). The distance from the center of the Rock to the Chuldah Tunnels is about 520 feet. According to the Shiltai HaGiborim the distance from the Holy of Holies to the

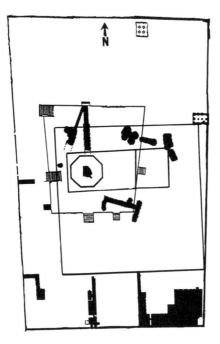

Plate 101. Location of the rectangular Azarah and the large square Har HaBayis, assuming the Rock to be the site of the Holy of Holies.

Southern Temple wall was 332.5 cubits. If 332.5 cubits equals 520 feet, then one cubit is about 1.564 feet, or 18.77 inches.

The distance to the eastern wall from the center of the Holy of Holies, according to the Shiltai HaGiborim, was 399 cubits. If one cubit is 1.564 feet, then 399 cubits equals 624 feet. Measured eastward from the center of the rock, the eastern wall of the Temple Compound is exactly 624 feet away.

We now know that the southern wall could not have been located farther south because then the length of a cubit would be more than 1.564 feet. If a cubit is more than 1.564 feet, then the eastern wall would be located farther eastward, placing it outside the Temple Compound, which is impossible.

According to the Shiltai HaGiborim, the distance to the north was 167.5 cubits, which equals 262 feet, and the distance to the western wall was 101 cubits, which equals 158 feet. In Plate 101 the walls of the Temple are shown, together with the walls of the Azarah and Women's Courtyard.

33

The Secret Passageway

Before the destruction of the First Temple in 420 B.C.E., the prophet Jeremiah hid the national treasures of the Jews under the Holy Temple to prevent them from falling into the hands of the invading Nebuchadnezzar and his Babylonian troops. The treasures included the Holy Ark, the Two Tablets with the Ten Commandments carved upon them, the staff of Aaron, the oil for annointing compounded by Moses, and a container holding the last sample of the manna that sustained the Children of Israel during their forty years of wandering through the desert. After the seventy years of the Babylonian exile, the Jews returned to Zion, but, alas, the treasures were never found.

The Mishna (Shekalim 6:1) records that the Holy Ark was hidden in a secret passageway that began beneath the Chamber of Wood, which was located in the northeastern corner of the Women's Courtyard. In Plate 101 we see that there is an underground room, marked "12," in that corner. It is a chamber forty-four feet below ground level, and has a vaulted ceiling. It has never been explored. Could this be the passageway that contains the hidden Ark and the Two Tablets? Of all the treasures yet to be discovered, what could be more important, more fascinating, and more awe-inspiring than the Tablets of the Ten Commandments? No other archeological find would have a greater impact on the destiny of man. These Tablets are the foundation of the three major religions. What a religious resurgence their discovery would cause. How it would cause scholars and laymen to reevaluate the past, examine the present, and speculate on the future cannot be imagined. Is it possible that such a sacred treasure lies but a few feet beneath what our eyes can see? Jewish tradition has always maintained that the treasures will remain hidden until the coming of the Messiah. Muslim tradition forbids the site from being explored. Curiosity is nature's most powerful force. Tradition is God's immovable object of faith. Here on the Temple Mount we find the answer to that ancient conundrum, "What happens when an irresistible force meets an immovable object?" for the treasures are yet to be discovered.

Other spots on the Temple Mount are also worthy of consideration. According to the Rosh, the Chamber of Wood was located outside the Women's Courtyard. Accordingly, the chamber beneath would then be the underground room marked "13" on the map. That room is forty feet below ground level. The three chambers, "12, 13, and 14" seem to be linked underground.

Careful examination of the Mishna text shows that the name Chamber of Wood is not used. The term the Mishna does employ is Wood Pen. Although the Rav says they are synonymous, it is possible that the reference is to something else. Earlier we mentioned that, according to some opinions (Plate 76, #26), along the southern side of the Azarah near the Firewood Gate was a room where the High Priest resided during the seven days prior to Yom Kippur. The room was called the Wood Chamber because wood was stored there during the rest of the year. Possibly, it is that room to which the Mishna refers as the hiding place of the Ark. If so, it would be in the vicinity of the underground tunnel marked "5." This chamber is forty-eight feet below ground level. Cut into the rock at the eastern end is a low doorway that leads to a flight of steps. The steps ascend toward the south, then sharply eastward. This eastward passage is covered by semicircular vaulting, and at the end are the remains of another doorway. A few feet beyond the doorway the opening is blocked by earth. This was the way Charles Wilson described the chamber in 1865.

34

The Altar Theory

Using the Shiltai HaGiborim's figures, we have been able to construct the possible location of the Azarah, the walls of the Holy Temple, and three possible locations of the hidden Holy Ark. We also have determined that a cubit is approximately 18.77 inches.

Let us reexamine the figures of the Shiltai HaGiborim. This time let us assume the rock to be the site of the Altar (see p. 143).

5. From the center of the Altar to the northern wall of the Azarah was 76.5 cubits.

6. From the center of the Altar to the southern wall of the Azarah was 58.5 cubits.

7. From the center of the Altar to the eastern wall of the Azarah was 38 cubits.

8. From the center of the Altar to the western wall of the Azarah was 149 cubits.

(Based on Mishna Midos)

According to the Shiltai HaGiborim, the distance from the northern wall of the Azarah to the northern wall of the Temple was 100 cubits (Figure A). Therefore, the distance from the center of the Altar to the northern wall of the Temple was 176.5 cubits (Figure A plus Figure 5). The distance from the southern wall of the Azarah to the southern wall of the Temple was 265 cubits (Figure B). Therefore, the distance from the center of the Altar to the southern wall of the Temple was 323.5 cubits (Figure B plus Figure 6). The distance from the eastern wall of the Azarah to the eastern wall of the Temple was 250 cubits (Figure C). Therefore, the distance from the center of the Altar to the eastern wall of the Temple was 288 cubits (Figure C plus Figure 7). The distance from the western wall of the Azarah to the western wall of the Temple was 63 cubits (Figure D). Therefore, the distance from the center of the Altar to the western wall of the Temple was 212 cubits (Figure D plus Figure 8).

As the southern wall of the Temple included the southern Chuldah Gates, we place the southern wall of the Temple at that point. Since it is 520 feet from the rock and that distances is 323.5 cubits, one cubit equals 1.6 feet or 19.29 inches. Plate 102 shows how the Temple walls and the Azarah would appear if the rock were the center of the Altar. The Holy of Holies turns out to be located on the western steps leading up to the Dome of the Rock platform. This fits in with the words of the Radak, who said that non-Jews would never build a structure over the Holy of Holies (Radak, Isaiah 64:10).

According to this reconstruction, the western wall of the Temple

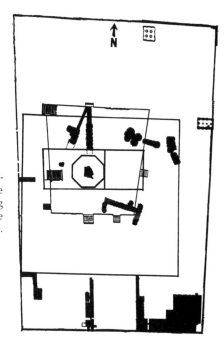

Plate 102. Location of the rectangular Azarah and the large square Har HaBayis, assuming the Rock to be the site of the Altar.

joins the western wall of Herod's extension toward the south. Because of this, we can say that the size of a cubit, for this calculation, cannot exceed 19.29 inches. Otherwise, part of the western wall of the Temple would be located outside the Temple compound.

It is useful to note that all the calculations we have made are taken from the center of the rock. The rock is 43 feet from east to west, and 57 feet from north to south. That gives us some room in which to modify our calculations. Also, all the calculations based on the archeological map are approximate, leaving some margin for error (probably no more than 5 percent).

The western wall of the Temple Mount was not only the western Temple wall, but its northern section was also the western wall of the Antonia Fortress. Josephus tells us that the western Antonia wall was equal to half the length of the western Temple wall. In these previous two reconstructions, this has been true.

The Tosfos Yom Tov (Midos 2:1) gives other figures for the distances between the walls of the Azarah and the walls of the Temple. However, he claims that the figures are only for illustrative purposes, and are not to be taken as law. I will simply mention his figures.

According to the Tosfos Yom Tov the distance between the southern wall of the Azarah and the southern wall of the Temple was 250 cubits; the distance between the northern wall of the Azarah and the northern wall of the Temple was 115 cubits; the distance between the eastern wall of the Azarah and the eastern wall of the Temple was 213 cubits; and the distance between the western wall of the Azarah and the western wall of the Temple was 100 cubits.

35

The Platform
of the Dome

The Dome of the Rock is built on an elevated platform, trapezoidal in shape. The walls around the Temple Mount also are trapezoidal, but that is because the outer walls follow the contour of the mountain and the surrounding valleys. Why does the platform of the Dome have such an awkward shape? Earlier, we mentioned that Herod's original plan was to create an elevated platform to serve as a foundation for the Temple. That platform was to be square or rectangular, but, as Josephus reported, parts of this foundation crumbled. This occurred on the eastern and western sides of the platform. The northern and southern sides are almost parallel, indicating that the northern and southern boundaries of the platform as it stands today are probably the northern and southern extent of the original flooring. We can therefore reconstruct the original platform as it was, or as it was supposed to have been. The northern and southern sides are still intact. The distance from north to south is about 550 feet. Adding the western and eastern parts that have collapsed, the distance from east to west must have been 540 feet.

The question to be raised is, what is that platform? It is most probably some floor level of the Temple, but which floor level? The central Temple floor level was the Azarah. The Azarah was 187 by 135 cubits, about 280 by 200 feet. The platform of the Dome is too large to be a remnant of the Azarah. The outer courtyard of the Temple Mount was 500 by 500 cubits, about 750 by 750 feet. The platform is too small to be the floor of the outer Temple courtyard. If the platform is too large to be the Azarah and too small to be the outer courtyard, what is it?

36

Rabban Gamaliel's Sacrifice

After the destruction of the Holy Temple in 70 c.e., sacrifices were no longer offered. The sacrificial rites could only be performed on the Altar, and the Altar had been destroyed.

One of the sacrifices brought during the years of the Temple was the Pascal sacrifice. Every year, on Passover eve, Jews made the pilgrimage to Jerusalem to offer the Pascal sacrifice. The meat was served on Passover night at the seder.

One of the unique characteristics of this sacrifice was the fact that it had to be roasted directly over a fire. It could not be cooked or fried like other sacrificial meat. There arose a rabbinic dispute as to whether the Pascal lamb could be roasted over a metal grill. Some rabbis permitted the practice; others said that the portion of the meat that came in contact with the metal grill would be fried by the heat of the metal, not roasted directly over the fire.

The Talmud records this dispute. One of the talmudic rabbis sought to resolve the matter concerning the use of a metal grill from the fact that Rabban Gamaliel, the illustrious sage, ordered his own servant to roast the Pascal sacrifice on a metal grill (Pesachim 74a). It is quite evident from the Talmud that Rabban Gamaliel lived during the Temple Era when the service of the Pascal sacrifice was still being performed.

However, Rabban Gamaliel was the grandfather of Judah the Prince, who compiled his magnum opus, the Mishna, in 220 C.E. How is it possible, then, that his grandfather offered a Pascal sacrifice 150 years earlier? Rabban Gamaliel was no youngster when he offered his sacrifice. He was already a renowned scholar with attending servants. How could he have offered a sacrifice?

37

Bar Kokhba's Temple

The two preceding chapters end with questions. One has baffled talmudic scholars and the other has perplexed archeologists, but more questions abound. They concern the life and times of Bar Kokhba.

One of the most enigmatic periods in Jewish history took place sixty years after the destruction of the Second Temple. In the year 130 C.E., the Jewish leader Shimon bar Kosiba led a rebellion against the Roman conquerors. Bar Kosiba recaptured Jerusalem and ruled as king for two and a half years (Sanhedrin 97b, Doros HaRishonim vol. 4, chap. 31). The illustrious talmudic sage, Rabbi Akiva, believing that the Messianic era was approaching, proclaimed Bar Kosiba as the Messiah. The rabbi changed Bar Kosiba's name to Bar Kokhba, the Son of the Star. Other rabbis, unconvinced of Bar Kosiba's integrity, called him Bar Koziba, the Son of Deceit. Bar Kosiba, quite understandably, followed the opinion of Rabbi Akiva, and proclaimed himself as the Messiah (Taanis 4:5).

Bar Kokhba issued coins on which he had inscribed, "Freedom for Israel." Many of these coins depict a temple facade (Plate 103). This type of depiction was very common on Roman coins of that era. But the Roman coins always showed a temple facade that was standing—a facade that was recognizable to anyone who had seen both the particular temple and the coin. Why would Bar Kokhba issue coins of a Jewish temple that had been destroyed sixty years earlier, a temple that was no longer standing, a temple whose facade would not be recognized?

Bar Kokhba appointed a High Priest and some of the coins include his name, Eleazer the Priest. The High Priest was the highest Temple official. He presided over the Temple service. If there was no Temple, there was no service. Why then did Bar Kokhba appoint a High Priest?

A primary function of the Jewish Messiah is to rebuild the Holy Temple as described in the Book of Ezekiel (Ezekiel 40–47). Since Bar Kokhba believed himself to be the Messiah, why didn't he at least begin rebuilding the Temple of the Jews during his two-and-a-half-year reign?

These questions almost suggest their own obvious solution. Bar Kokhba did in fact rebuild the Temple during the years he ruled in Jerusalem. The Temple required a High Priest, a position that was filled by the appointment of Eleazer. The Temple facade that Bar Kokhba built was represented on the Bar Kokhba coins. Bar Kokhba was so convinced that his conquest of Jerusalem heralded the beginning of the Messianic era that he began a new calendar system of counting the years from the date of his conquest. The coins are stamped "year one," "year two," and "year three." Rabban Gamaliel, who lived during the Bar Kokhba revolution, offered his Pascal sacrifice in the Bar Kokhba Temple.

All our questions have been answered, except one. Which

Plate 103. A Bar Kokhba coin depicting the facade of the Holy Temple.

flooring of the Temple is the 550-foot by 540-foot Dome of the Rock platform? We shall now address that question.

A description of the Second Temple is discussed throughout the Talmud and in a specially designated tractate, Midos. Josephus Flavius, in his two works, *Jewish Antiquities* and *The Jewish War*, also gives us a description of the Second Temple. Josephus mentions his intention to write a separate treatise on the Temple structure. Either the work was never written or it has been lost. In any event, we do not have that work. The Messianic Third Temple is described in the book of Ezekiel. The Third Temple is radically different from the Second Temple. In the Second Temple, to the east of the inner Azarah Courtyard was an area designated for women called the Women's Courtyard. It was 135 cubits square, or 202½ feet by 202½ feet, assuming a cubit to be 1½ feet. To the west of the Women's Courtyard was the Azarah Courtyard, 202½ feet from north to south and 280½ feet from east to west. The two courtyards formed a rectangle 202½ feet wide and 483 feet long. In Ezekiel's Third Temple the Women's Courtyard was a much larger area, almost square (Plate 104). It was 346 cubits north to south by 340 cubits east to west, or about 519 feet by 510 feet (Tzuras HaBayis, Ezekiel). The Azarah Courtyard was contained within the surrounding Women's Courtyard.

We have been assuming that a cubit is about 18 inches. That is only an approximation based on an educated guess. What if a cubit is 19 inches, or, more precisely, 19.07 inches? Then the dimensions of the Messianic Temple would be 550 feet by 540 feet. Those are exactly the same dimensions of the Dome of the Rock platform!

We now have mathematical evidence that the Dome of the Rock platform is the remains of the Bar Kokhba Messianic Temple. As an additional bonus, we can calculate the size of a cubit to be 19.07 inches.

Maimonides describes the Women's Courtyard as an elevated floor surrounded by a retaining wall, called the Cheil, from the Hebrew word cheil, "to give strength." The Cheil, Maimonides states, was 10 cubits high. The Dome of the Rock platform is elevated and is surrounded by a wall about 15 feet high. The height varies, but it would seem that the wall around the Dome platform is Maimonides' Cheil.

In the Messianic Third Temple, the altar occupied the center position of the sacred area (HaMikdash HaShilishi). The altar was 32 cubits long, 32 cubits wide, and 10 cubits high. Assuming a cubit to be 19.07 inches, the altar occupied a square area of 50.85 feet on

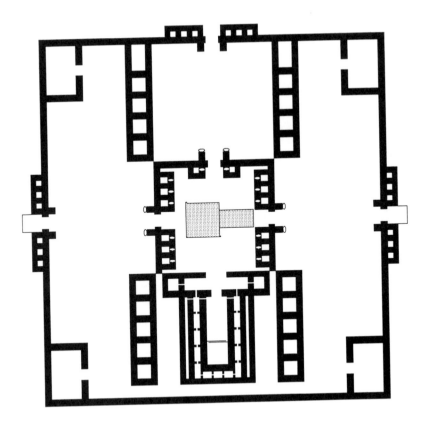

Plate 104. Ezekiel's Third Temple.

each side. The Holy of Holies was 111 cubits to the west, about 176 feet. A glance at the diagram of the Dome of the Rock platform (see Plate 36) shows the rock to be a few feet southwest of center. Therefore, it appears that the rock is associated with the altar, and the site of the Holy of Holies was 176 feet to the west, near the western steps that lead up to the platform. This contention has been stated in earlier chapters, see particularly Chapter 23, "The Dome of the Rock and the Shis."

In Chapter 34, "The Altar Theory," and in Plate 102, I presented a reconstruction of the Second Temple assuming the rock to be the site of the Altar. It was also determined that a cubit was approximately equal to 19.29 inches. In this chapter, I am assuming the platform of the Dome of the Rock to be the flooring of the Messianic Third Temple, and again the rock is found to be the site of the Altar and a cubit about 19.07 inches. The figures are close enough to give the theories statistical validity.

If my theories are valid, then the following have been demonstrated:

1. We have new perspective of Messianic implications of the Bar Kokhba era.

2. There is a better understanding of the depiction and inscriptions of the Bar Kokhba coins.

3. The platform of the Dome of the Rock is the remains of the Messianic Temple.

4. The Rock is the site of the Sacrificial Altar.

5. A cubit is between 19.07 and 19.29 inches.

6. It is possible to locate and reconstruct the Second Temple on top of the Temple Mount with some degree of accuracy.

The concept that the Jews began building the Messianic Temple is quite revolutionary. I am not certain of its theological implications. However, subsequent to writing this, I have seen in the writings of the nineteenth-century Lithuanian talmudic commentary of Rabbi Samuel Shtrashun, known as R'shash, in his work on Pesachim 74a, the suggestion that Rabban Gamaliel offered his Pascal sacrifice on the altar of a Messianic Bar Kokhba Temple. He bases his assumption on the words of a noted Roman historian of the period, probably Dio Casius.

38

The Destruction
of the Third Temple

Bar Kokhba reigned as the Messiah-king in Jerusalem for two and a half years. However, the dream of Rabbi Akiva and the Jewish people was not realized. When the Roman emperor Hadrian captured the Holy City, Bar Kokhba and the citizens of the Judean capital fled to Betar. Hadrian converted the Messianic Temple into a temple of pagan worship dedicated to Jupiter. Jerusalem was renamed Aelia Capitolina; the city of the Messiah was now a Roman garrison (Doros HaRishonim).

The Romans besieged Betar for three and a half years. In the end Betar fell, resulting in a horrendous bloodbath in which Bar Kokhba was also killed—by the Jews. The man who once was proclaimed the Messiah suffered from egomania and paranoia. He pleaded with God not to interfere with his plans. "Do not help me; do not hinder me," Bar Kokhba cried out. He suspected everyone of betrayal. Bar Kokhba murdered the great sage, Rabbi Elazar of Modiim, accusing him of treason. In the end, the Jews betrayed Bar Kokhba (Sanhedrin 93b; Taanis 4:5).

39

The Apostate Gives
the Messiah Another Chance

In 135 C.E., Hadrian converted the Temple into a center for paganism. That status remained for almost 200 years. In 324 Emperor Constantine converted to Christianity and moved the seat of the Roman Empire to Byzantium. Jerusalem became a holy Christian city. The Emperor's mother, Helena, had many churches and shrines erected in Jerusalem. Jews were forbidden entrance to the city, except on the Ninth day of Av, in order to mourn their loss. The pagan temple on the mount was torn down. The mountain was now desolate and bare.

In 363, a new emperor, Julian, was crowned. Although raised as a Christian, he grew up in the pagan city of Athens, and upon assuming the throne, renounced Christianity. He was branded Julian the Apostate by the Christian faithful. He granted full rights to the Jews and gave them permission to restore the Temple.

At once, the Jews in the Holy Land began assembling supplies in great storehouses. Messianic hopes were stirred. But alas, a great earthquake tore down the storehouses, destroying the supplies. Within the year Julian was killed in battle and the new emperor, Jovian, restored Christianity as the religion of the realm. Again the hopes of the Jews for the long awaited Messiah were dashed.

40

And Your Hearts Shall Rejoice

Toward the beginning of the seventh century, the Persians, with the help of the Jews, captured Jerusalem. The Persian king, Chosroes II, appointed a Jew named Nehemiah as governor of the Holy City. The Jews were given permission to rebuild their Temple. The Christian inhabitants began civil unrest. Under pressure, the Persians withdrew the favored status bestowed upon the Jewish citizens.

Fifteen years later, in 629 C.E., the Byzantine emperor, Heraclius, recaptured Jerusalem. Filled with the spirit of revenge against the Jews, the Christian Byzantines began building an octagonal church

Plate 105. During the seventh century, a Jew carved a verse from Isaiah on the Western Wall. It says, "And you shall see, and your hearts shall rejoice and your bones [shall spring forth] like the grass." It expresses hope for the messianic redemption and the resurrection of the dead. The story behind the carving is found on page 162.

Plate 105A. For 2,000 years the Jews have embraced the holy stones of the Wailing Wall and have prayed for the coming of the Messiah and the rebuilding of the Temple.

atop the Temple Mount. Although the Mount had no special sanctity to the Christians, "defiling" the Temple Mount with a church would be the ultimate insult to the Jews and dash their hopes of ever regaining the holy mountain.

The Byzantine church was never completed. In 637 c.e. the Muslims captured the Holy Land and the church was converted into the Muslim shrine, the Dome of the Rock.

During the brief Persian era, a Jewish passerby engraved a verse on the western Herodian wall, based on the prophecy of Isaiah: "And you shall see, and your hearts shall rejoice; for your bones like the grass shall spring forth" (Isaiah 66:14). The verse was never completed. The words "shall spring forth" are missing. It is as though the engraver was interrupted during his work. Also, the carved verse reads "their bones" instead of the correct "your bones." The engraved prophecy refers to the Messianic era, when the dead shall be resurrected and rise up from the ground like the grasses. No doubt the engraver felt that the beginning of the End of Days was at hand. The Messiah was about to come. Redemption. The resurrection of the dead.

The engraver's hopes were not realized. The engraver has long since died, but his verse is still there today, to the left of Robinson's Arch (Plate 105). The yearning prophecy of hope still calls forth from the wall.

"Rejoice ye with Jerusalem and be delighted over her. Be glad with her all those who mourned for her" (Isaiah 66:10).

And Your Hearts Shall Rejoice **163**

A APPENDIX

Yoseph ben Gurion

Perhaps the most famous nonrabbinical source of information concerning the Holy Temple comes from the writings of Yoseph ben Gurion. He is known as Josephus Flavius or Yosiphon. He was born in 37 C.E. and died in 100 C.E. Josephus came from a priestly family and claimed descent from the house of the Hasmoneans, although the Talmud states that all the descendants of the Hasmoneans were killed in the time of Herod (Baba Basra 3a). Some say Josephus was the brother of the Nakdimon ben Gurion mentioned in the Talmud (Taanis 20a; Gittin 56a).

Between the ages of 16 and 19, Josephus was tutored by three different sects, the Essenes (Issiyim), the Pharisees (Pairushim), and the Sadducees (Tzaddukim). Josephus's own description of these three sects tells us where his faith and philosophy lay.

> The Essenes are known for their extreme piousness and saintliness. They show greater mutual respect than do other sects. They hold pleasure to be a vice and temperance as a virtue. They disdain marriage, but adopt other people's children while young, molding them in their own ways. They do not condemn marriage in principle, but desire to protect themselves against woman's unfaithfulness.
>
> They hold wealth in contempt. All new members must surrender their property so that no poverty nor wealth is seen. Each man's possessions become part of the group's resources. They regard oils and perfumes as polluting. They all wear

white. They choose officers to supervise the affairs of the community. The responsibility of each officer is decided by vote.

The sect settles in great numbers in every town. When followers arrive from elsewhere, they place their resources at the guest's disposal. They entertain the men whom they had never known as though they were best of friends.

When they travel, they carry no baggage, only weapons to ward off robbers. In every community one officer oversees that new arrivals have clothing and provisions. Clothing and shoes are not changed until they are worn out and tattered. Nothing is sold or bought from amongst themselves, but everyone gives to those in need.

Before sunrise no one utters a word regarding secular affairs. In prayer they beseech God to make Himself known. Afterwards, they engage in crafts for which they have a reputation. At the fifth hour they bathe in cold water, put on their sacred garments, and assemble in a private hall. No one is allowed to enter the hall except the initiated.

Everyone takes his seat in silence. A baker serves them loaves of bread and a cook sets before each one a prepared food. The priest says a blessing, none may eat before the prayer. After eating, another blessing is recited. The meal commences with a blessing and ends with a blessing, giving honor to God as the giver of life. They remove their sacred garments and return to their work.

When they return in the evening, they resume eating in the same manner as before. The serving of meat and the drinking of wine is curtailed. They speak softly, each in his turn. To outsiders the softness of tones seems like some awesome mystery.

Giving of presents is forbidden unless approved by an official. They keep tempers under control. Every word they utter is as binding as an oath. For a man who is not believed, they hold, is condemned. They are devoted to the study of ancient books, mostly those that benefit the body and soul. They search out medicinal roots and healing stones.

One who desires to join the sect must remain an outsider for one year. During that time he must abide by the rules. He is given a hatchet, a loin cloth, and a set of white garments. When he has shown his temperance, he is admitted closer into the fold, sharing in the waters of sanctification, but cannot participate in the meetings. Only after two years, if he has demonstrated his strength of character and determination, then he is admitted into the society.

Men convicted of major offenses are expelled from the order. They are bound by oath not to seek assistance else-where. And so they are reduced to eating grass and weeds. Eventually the body wastes and dies of starvation. Many offenders have been taken back at their last gasp for breath. They feel any man who suffers to the point of death has sufficiently paid for his misdeeds.

They are just and scrupulously careful in trying court cases. Sentence is never passed in a tribunal of less than a hundred. After God, they hold Moses in great esteem; whoever curses the name of Moses is punished by death. With regards to the Sabbath they are stricter than all Jews. They move no vessel on the holy day, nor do they relieve themselves.

They are divided into four classes according to the duration of their training. If a senior member is touched by an inferior member, the senior must immerse himself in a mikva as though he were contaminated by a heathen. They are long lived, most passing the century mark. They owe this, I believe, to their simple and regular manner of life. They despise danger and conquer pain by the will of the mind. Their spirit was tested to the utmost by the Romans. The Romans tortured and burned them, using every instrument of terror to make them blaspheme their lawgiver or to eat some forbidden food. The sect did not yield nor shed a tear. Rejoicing in their agony, they mocked their tormentors. Cheerfully they resigned their souls, confident they would receive it back again.

They have an unshakable belief in the corruptibility of the body and in the immortality of the soul. They believe the soul is rewarded or punished according to the life one lived.

Some claim to tell the future as a result of lifelong study of sacred writings. Rarely do their predictions prove wrong.

There is a second order of Essenes which agrees with the way of life, customs, and regulations of the first. They differ only with their view to marriage. Marriage, according to them, is a most sacred duty, for without it, the race would disappear. A bride to be is put on three years probation. They have no intercourse during pregnancy to show that marriage is not for pleasure but to propagate the race. When women immerse themselves, they wear a dress just as the men wear a loincloth. Such are the customs of this order.

The next sect, the Pharisees, are held to be the most accurate interpreters of the law and are the leading sect. They hold that man has the free will to choose right or wrong, but in every action fate has a share. Every soul is immortal. The souls of the good pass into another body. The souls of the wicked are condemned to suffer eternal punishment.

The Sadducees deny fate altogether. God, they believe, cannot see sin. They deny the immortality of the soul and the idea of reward and retribution in a future world. The Pharisees are friendly to one another and cultivate harmony with the community. The Sadducees show a disagreeable behavior even in their relations to each other. [*The Jewish War*, Book 2, chap. 8]

From the description Josephus gives of the three sects we can see his admiration for the Essenes. His detailed elaboration makes us suspect that the sect was not widely known outside Judea. In modern times, interest in the group was rekindled with the discovery of the Dead Sea Scrolls, which have been attributed to the Essenes. One of the Scrolls, called the Temple Scroll, deals exclusively with the Temple (but that is another story, which is why I include Josephus's account of the Essenes).

Josephus's disdain for the Sadducees is obvious, even from this short account. Although he considered himself a Pharisee, Josephus provides little in the way of description of their beliefs and customs. Because they were a well-known sect, probably no elaboration was necessary.

At age 29, Josephus was appointed general over the Galilean troops engaged in fighting the Romans. He had over 100,000 foot soldiers and 5,000 riders under his command. Josephus blamed the radical Zealots for political turmoil and the necessity of fighting Rome. He believed them to be warmongers, and held them directly responsible for the eventual destruction of the Temple and the Holy City.

With the fall of the stronghold of Jotapata, Josephus fled with scores of his comrades and hid in a cave. The Romans discovered their hiding place and offered to allow them to surrender peacefully. Josephus was in favor, but his troops were opposed. They preferred committing suicide to becoming Roman slaves. Because of the troops' opposition, Josephus agreed to a mass suicide pact. Soldiers drew lots to determine who would slay the first man. Josephus knew how to arrange the drawing so that he and a sympathetic companion would be the last to live. After the troops killed one another, Josephus and his companion, the only survivors, surrendered, claiming that suicide was against their religious principles.

From that point on, Josephus was a pacifist. He accompanied the Roman troops, urging his countrymen to lay down their arms and allay their hostile attitude. He adopted the surname Flavius, after the Roman emperor Vespasian. Josephus frequently wrote that he would have met with success had it not been for the diabolical schemes of the Zealots. Josephus felt that these radicals were on a suicide course, and that they took the city and the Temple with them.

During the siege of Jerusalem, Josephus began recording material for his books. He wrote his first book in Aramaic, so that his countrymen, even those far away in Africa and Asia, would know in detail the calamity that had befallen the Jewish nation. In 76 C.E., when he was 49 years old, the book was completed. Later it was translated into Hebrew, and that is the book that today we call *Yosiphon*, Josephus's Aramaic name.

After he completed the Aramaic version, he had associates assist him in a Greek version of the book. He called it *The Jewish War*. It commences with the Maccabean revolt, and ends with the march of triumph in Rome celebrating the defeat of Judea. The two books differ greatly. Both were subject to additions, deletions, and revisions by copyists. Scholastic battles waged as to which version was the more reliable.

In 93 C.E., Josephus wrote *Jewish Antiquities*, a history of the Jewish people from creation until 66 C.E. It consisted of twenty books. This is the primary secular source for the history of the Jews. In addition, Josephus wrote an autobiography, an account of the Hasmonean dynasty, and *Against Apion*—a discourse against those who claim that the Jews possess no history or claim to antiquity. Josephus tells us that he planned to write a book on the Temple; however, it has been lost, or was never actually begun.

The books of Josephus, including *Yosiphon*, are not sacred books. They have not been subject to careful scrutiny over the centuries. There are contradictions between *Antiquities* and *The Jewish War*. There are also contradictions and different accounts between *Yosiphon* and the other two books. On occasion, Josephus's halachic rulings are incorrect, along with his relating of philosophies. How much of that is due to his lack of knowledge, lack of consistency, inaccuracy as an observer, orthographical errors, or the whims of later copyists is not known. None of this, however, diminishes the uniqueness of his accounts, or the value of studying his writings.

Yosiphon's Temple

In Chapter 55 of *Yosiphon*, Josephus gives a description of the Second Temple (Plate 106). I feel it not only useful but important to quote from his text and annotate where necessary.

Plate 106. Hizkiyahu's Pool. This cistern is located to the north of the Fortress of David. In ancient times it served as a water supply for the Herodian Fortress and King's Palace to the south.

"The house that King Herod built was 100 cubits in length, 100 cubits in width, and 120 cubits high." This reference is to the Heichel, which the Mishna describes as 100 cubits long and 100 cubits wide (Midos 4:6). However, the Mishna states that the Heichel was also 100 cubits high, whereas *Yosiphon* says that it was 120 cubits high. In 2 Chronicles 3:4 the height of the First Temple is given as 120 cubits. The prophet Haggai says that the glory of the Second Temple will be greater than that of the First (Haggai 2:9). This has always been interpreted to mean that the Second Temple will be larger than the First (Baba Basra 3a). If that is so, how can the first Heichel be 120 cubits high and second only 100 cubits? The explanation is that the height of 120 cubits was from the base of the building to the top of the roof (Rashi, 2 Chronicles 3:4). The height of 100 cubits, mentioned in connection with the second Heichel, is the height of the walls around the structure to the bottom of the upward-sloping roof. The height of the second Heichel together with the roof was also 120 cubits.

In the First Temple (Plate 107), the height of the Kodesh was only 30 cubits. In the Second Temple, the height of the Kodesh was 40 cubits (Baba Basra 3a). Although the height of both exteriors was 120 cubits, the inside height of the Kodesh of the Second Temple was greater than that of the first.

"Only the interior of the structure he raised, that was within the roof of the house, its height was 20 cubits." This phrase is very unclear. "Besides this, the foundation of 20 cubits was below. This

Plate 107. The Tomb of Zecharyah. Some say it is the tomb of the prophet, Zecharyah; others say it is the tomb of a First Temple High Priest, Zecharyah, who was murdered in the Temple by his fellow Jews because of his admonitions to them. The tomb is carved out of one solid piece of rock (see Plate 16).

is the account of the height." The Mantua edition of *Yosiphon* reads, ". . . the foundation of 10 cubits below." The Mishna (Midos 4:6) states that the foundation was 6 cubits. Earlier we discussed the fact that the Heichel's 6-cubit foundation rested upon a platform, which was 20 cubits high (see Chapter 19). The elevated platform served as the floor of the Azarah. This is the foundation to which Josephus refers. Maimonides stated that the Cheil was a 10-cubit-high retaining wall that held up the platform. According to Maimonides, the Mantua text, referring to an elevation of 10 cubits, would be more correct.

"The stones which the king used to construct the house were white as snow. The length of each stone was 25 cubits, the width was 12 cubits, and its height 8 cubits, stones of marble. One measure for all the stones, from the bottom of the house until its edge. And it was raised very high in the middle of the city, and could be seen from afar."

Yosiphon says that the width of the stones was 12 cubits. Nowhere do we find walls with a 12-cubit thickness. In fact, the thickest wall was only 6 cubits. Also, *Yosiphon* describes the stones as "white as snow." The Talmud (Baba Basra 4a) says, "It was said, 'Whoever has not seen the building of Herod, has never seen a beautiful building.' Of what did he build it? Rabbah said, 'Of yellow and white marble.' Some say, 'Of blue, yellow, and white marble.' The rows alternated. One row was set in, the next set out, in order to hold the cement. He thought to cover it with gold, but the sages advised him not to, for it was more beautiful as it was, looking like the waves of the sea." *Yosiphon*'s white stones are the blocks used to construct the Heichel. The Talmud's blue, yellow, and white stones are probably the flooring or the walls of the Azarah.

"And the king leveled all around the house. He leveled all the slopes and surrounded the house with four halls." Herod "leveled" the slope of the mountain by building three levels of vaults along its side. The upper vault supported the floor of the Temple. The vaults not only helped to support the floor above, but also served to separate any possible gravesite in the mountain and the Temple. As the Mishna (Para: 33) says, "The Temple and the courtyards were hollow underneath because of gravesites below." "A bridge was built from the Temple Mount to the Mount of Anointing, vaults upon vaults, and vaults upon the foundation pillars" (Para 3:6). The Rambam (Bais HaB'chirah 5) explains that vaults upon vaults were also beneath the floors of the Temple.

"And he built an eastern hall and placed it eastward. The hall faced the house and its back was to the east. Its length was 250 cubits, its width 100 cubits, like the measure of the house, and its height was 120 cubits. And he made a courtyard before the eastern hall built with marble flooring."

Where was this eastern hall located? We must realize that this was only one of four identical halls, which Josephus will soon describe. Four halls 100 cubits by 250 cubits could not fit into the Azarah, which was only 135 cubits by 187 cubits. Obviously they were located outside the Azarah, but according to the Shiltai HaGiborim, there were only 63 cubits between the western wall of the Azarah and the western wall of the Temple. How could a hall 100 cubits wide fit into a space of 63 cubits? We will have to assume that, according to the Shiltai HaGiborim, the halls were located in the Herodian extension. Although these halls are not mentioned in any of the talmudic writings, they are mentioned by the most revered and respected biblical and talmudic commentator, Rashi (Rashi, Rosh HaShana 23a, "Kol").

"He made 160 columns in four rows. Forty columns in the first row. Forty columns in the second row. Forty columns in the third row, and forty columns in the fourth row. The length of a single column was 50 cubits. Its width was 3 cubits. The same measure for the 160 columns. Between the columns was 15 cubits. So it was until the end of the column structure."

It would seem that these rows of columns were inside the hall. This can be shown to be impossible. Each row had forty columns. Each column was 3 cubits wide. The space between the columns was 15 cubits. The total length of each row of columns was 705 cubits. How could four rows of columns, each 705 cubits in length, be contained in a hall that was only 250 cubits long?

It therefore seems obvious that *Yosiphon* is describing something else. But what? Earlier, when we discussed the Herodian extension, we mentioned the Royal Basilica, the largest building in the Temple. I believe it is this structure that *Yosiphon* is describing. The Royal Basilica is described by Josephus (*Antiquities*, Book 15, chap. 11, para. 5) as follows:

> The fourth front of the Temple was southward, and it contained the Royal Basilica. It had three walkways which reached from the valley on the east to the valley on the west. It could go no further. This building deserves to be mentioned better than any under the sun, for while the valley was very deep, its bottom could not be seen if you looked from above into the depth. It stood upon such great heights, that if one looked down from the roof, he would become giddy, and his sight could not reach to such a great depth. This basilica had columns that stood in four rows, one opposite the other. The fourth row was interwoven with the [southern] wall. The thickness of each column was such that three men with their arms joined and extended could encircle it. The height of each column was 27 feet with a double spiral for a base. The total number of columns was 162. The capitals were of the Corinthian order and caused amazement to the spectators of such grandeur [Plate 108]. These four rows made three aisles for walking. The two outer aisles were 30 feet wide and a furlong in length. The height was 50 feet. The middle aisle was one and a half times wider and twice as high. The roofs were adorned with deep sculptures in wood representing many forms. The middle was much higher. The front wall was adorned with beams, resting upon pillars, that were set into the wall. The front was polished stone, its fineness had not been seen before. It was incredible; whoever saw it was greatly amazed.

The discrepancies between the two versions are many and obvious. It is not my intent to try to reconcile them. However, the similarities between the two accounts are also obvious. The space between the columns is 15 cubits. If we assume that the measure is

Plate 108. The capital of a Corinthian column that was tossed down from the Temple Mount to the street below.

taken from the middle of one column to the middle of the next, then there are 39 gaps between the 40 columns, each gap 15 cubits. That equals 585 cubits. Add the thickness of half the outer two columns, which was 3 cubits, and the total is 588 cubits. The building stretched along the southern length of the Temple, which was 922 feet. Each cubit comes to 1.568 feet or 18.82 inches, a reasonable length.

Segments of columns 4.9 feet wide have been unearthed near the base of the southern wall. *Yosiphon* says that the columns were 3 cubits thick. Since each cubit is 1.568 feet, 3 cubits would be 4.7 feet, a difference of a mere 2½ inches. That is quite acceptable as the columns were not bound by any Torah or rabbinical law to be exactly 3 cubits thick. It is assumed that the columns were thrown down by invaders from the Royal Basilica. The capitals were of the Corinthian order, and as the rule of classical Roman architecture was that the height of a Corinthian column was 10 times its width, that would make the columns about 49 feet high. The capitals of the columns supported pillars that supported the roof. When *Yosiphon* said that the columns were 50 cubits, or about 80 feet, high, perhaps he was including the upper pillars, which rested upon the lower pillars and supported the roof.

"The manner [length?] of the eastern courtyard was 27 cubits [720 cubits—Mantua edition], for the building reached until the Kidron valley [Plate 109]." One can only guess at the location of this courtyard.

Plate 109. Across from the Eastern Temple Wall, in the Kidron Valley, is Yad Avshalom. Avshalom, the rebellious son of King David, having no sons to succeed him, feared he would be forgotten. Legend says that Avshalom built this monument to himself to insure that future generations would remember him. His plan backfired. It became the custom for Jews, Arabs, and Christians to throw stones at the monument while saying, "So should be done to a son who rebels against his father." The lower two-thirds of the tomb is carved out of one solid piece of rock. In back to the left is the tomb of the Judean king Jehoshaphat. This part of the Kidron Valley is called the Valley of Jehoshaphat.

> He made vaults over the valley, and upon the vaults he built bridges and flooring of stone. And he built the structure upon them and fastened the structure. He raised up the structure greatly until the valley could not be seen from opposite the house. And he made three roofs. Joseph ben Gurion, the priest, [that is, Yosiphon, as authors commonly referred to themselves by name] said whoever stood upon the third roof, in those times, would be unable to see the bottom of the valley because of the great height of the structure, for only darkness was seen below. The bottom of the valley could not be seen.

Many phrases from this quotation are familiar to us. The third "roof" may refer to the top of the third vault. The inability of the viewer to see the bottom of the valley was mentioned before by Josephus.

> And the king built a wall of silver between the hall and the house. He fashioned a door of gold facing the house. He placed above the door a sword made from a talent of gold.

Engraved upon the sword was, 'The foreigner who approaches will die.'

And he made the southern hall, and placed it opposite the house southward, with its back to the south and its front to the house. Its length was 250 cubits and its width was 100 cubits, like the measure of the house, and its height was 120 cubits.

And he placed before [opposite?] it a courtyard, and the hall was above the yard. He closed up the yard and joined it to the eastern yard. And he made gateways and doors, just as he made for the eastern yard.

He made a hall in the west toward the setting of the sun. Its back to the west and its front toward the house. Its length was 250 cubits and its width 100 cubits, like the measure of the house, and its height was 120 cubits.

And he made in it four gateways. One gate looked toward the place of King Herod. There were three [other gate-] ways. Two led outside the city, and one led down by steps to the valley. From there one could go around and up to the city. For the city, together with the Temple, looked like a fortress surrounded by a deep valley.

Although *Yosiphon* does not mention a courtyard on the western side, later it does say that there were four courtyards, three of which had the same dimensions. The fourth was narrower.

And so he did in the northern courtyard just as he did in the southern courtyard. And he made a hall to the north and placed it north of the house. The hall, its back to the north and its front to the house. Its length 250 cubits and its width 100 cubits, like the measure of the house, and its height 120 cubits high. And he made a yard, and placed it before [opposite?] the northern hall. Its length 27 cubits and its width was like the width of the southern yard. The halls were all of the same measure, and the yards were all of the same measure. Only the fourth yard was not the same measure as the other three yards, for its place was narrow, and therefore the king did not lengthen it." *Yosiphon* does not state which yard is the fourth yard, but it refers to either the length of the southern yard, since the southern part of the compound was the shortest, or the western yard, which had the narrowest space.

The king made four gateways on the western side in the courtyard, four gateways to the south in the courtyard, four to the north in the courtyard, and in the eastern courtyard he placed twelve gateways and placed one great gateway there.

Josephus (*The Jewish War*, Book 5, chap. 5, para. 2) describes the Azarah, "whose gates on the north and south sides were eight, four on each side." Of necessity there were two on the east. One was used by women, since it was there they came to worship. This gate was cut out of the wall over against (opposite?) the first gate. The next section gives a more detailed description of the Temple by Josephus.

> This gateway we did not enter through it with our wives and children, only with sanctity and purity did we enter every time when we came in those days. Then we came and went upon the flooring that was in the courtyard before the hall that was before the house. [This refers to the courtyard of the Israelites.]
>
> And we came to the hall; however, the women did not come to it. We men did not approach the house, for it was the boundary of the priests. Even the priests did not approach the Holy of Holies except the High Priest who would come there one time in the year. However, all that was in the house we saw when we stood in the hall in those days. All the work of gold that was in the house we saw when the gate of the house was open to the yard. The golden cluster and all its works, and all the works of the house, and its gold ornaments that was from the booty of the nations that God gave into the hands of King Herod, and when He saved Israel from them. All were hanging on the walls of the house outside.
>
> And Joseph the priest, the son of Gorion the priest, spoke saying, 'All that we have told here we saw with our eyes and rejoiced in it. And afterwards there reached to us a great mourning, the destruction of the house, of which we are unable to relate but a small part.'
>
> The building was completed after eight years, and for all this we offered thankfulness and praises to God as befits Him. From the beginning of the building until its completion, God did not allow it to rain during the day in Jerusalem, in order not to hinder the building of the Heichel.
>
> So spoke Joseph the priest, the son of Gorion the priest, who testified to this according to the tradition of the sages of Israel and according to the reliable scribes of the nations.

The Josephus Temple

Josephus, in his *Jewish Antiquities* and *The Jewish War*, gives a description of the Temple. He describes other areas of the Temple not mentioned in the Aramaic version. I now quote Josephus's description of the Temple and make comments where appropriate.

"In the fifteenth year of his reign, Herod restored the Temple" (*The Jewish War*, Book 1, chap. 21).

In *Antiquities* (Book 15, chap. 11, para. 1), Josephus writes that the restoration occurred in the eighteenth year of Herod's reign.

"He enlarged the surrounding area to double its extent by erecting new supporting walls. The expenditure involved was tremendous and the result was magnificent beyond compare. This is exemplified by the large stoas around the Temple courts and the fortress which dominated it to the north. Herod constructed the stoas from their foundations" (*The Jewish War*, Book 1, chap. 21, para. 1, 401. The remainder of the quotes, with exceptions noted, are found in Book 5, chap. 5, para. 1–6).

A stoa is a series of columns running parallel to a wall. The columns support a roof going from the top of the columns to the adjacent wall.

"The Temple was built on a strong hill. The level area on its summit originally was hardly spacious enough for the Sanctuary and Altar, since the ground was steep. King Solomon, the actual founder of the Sanctuary [Plate 110], walled up the eastern side and erected a single portico on the built up ground." (**Note**: A portico is either a stoa or an area marked off before or behind a doorway. It can be marked off with walls, columns, or both. The term "portico" as used here could mean either.) "The other sides of

Plate 110. The Temple Wall had grooves built into it. These contained clay water pipes that led water from Solomon's Pools, outside of Bethlehem, into the Holy Temple.

Plate 111. A Muslim entrance into the Northern Temple Wall.
In Temple times the Tadi Gate was located nearby.

the Sanctuary remained exposed. In the course of time, a breach
was made in the northern wall [Plate 111] and an area was added
equal to the whole of the Temple. Then, the hill was closed off from
its base with a wall on three sides. This task staggered the
imagination, a task on which they spent an endless amount of time
and all their sacred treasures. Donations were sent from every
corner of the world as a gift to God. They built both the upper
courtyards and the lower courtyards around the original block."

Josephus begins by saying that there was only an eastern wall,
built by King Solomon. In the next sentence he refers to a northern
wall. Obviously, this northern wall was added after the time of
King Solomon. When Josephus says that "the hill was closed off
from its base with a wall on three sides," it is unclear if he was
refering to the area added to the northern side, which formed a
"hill," or to the entire mountain.

Earlier I mentioned a seam in the eastern Temple wall. The
stones to the south of the seam are typical Herodian ashlars. The
stones to the north of the seam have rough, protruding centers. It
may very well be that these stones are from the wall of Solomon's

eastern extension. If that is the case, then the area from the rock all the way to these stones would be sacred, as any extension to the sacred Temple area would have been built when a prophet and the Urim V'Tumim were still functioning, thus bestowing sanctity upon them. When the Herodian extension and its walls were built, there was no prophet, nor were there functioning Urim V'Tumim. The Herodian extensions therefore would have had no sanctity.

"They built the lower enclosure." (**Note**: "Lower enclosure" refers to the Herodian extension, as it was lower than the sacred precincts.) "Its foundations were the deepest, a depth of 300 cubits, and in some places even more." (**Note**: The retaining walls [Plate 112] of the lower enclosure went all the way down to bedrock.) "The depth of the foundations was not apparent, for they filled up the ravines for much of its height in order to make it level with the streets of the city below. Blocks of stone 40 cubits

Plate 112. A close-up of the retaining wall of the Dome of the Rock platform. From the sealed-up archways, it is obvious that under the platform were rooms and chambers. In medieval times they were used by Muslim pilgrims.

long were used in the building. Though there were lavish contributions and great enthusiasm, the task seemed endless and through perseverance it was completed after many years.

"The structures of the Sanctuary were worthy of such foundations. The stoas were erected in double rows and were supported by columns 25 cubits high, cut from single blocks of the purest white marble. The ceiling was paneled with cedar. The natural magnificence of these columns, their polish and accurate jointing, made a striking spectacle, without any added ornament of painting or carving. The stoas were 30 cubits wide and the complete length all around was six furlongs, the Antonia tower being included. From end to end, the open courtyard was paved with all manner of different stones."

In *Antiquities*, Josephus gives the total length of the stoas as four furlongs. Obviously, he was not including the stoas of the Antonia. We must conclude that the stoa went around the entire Temple Compound, including the Antonia. A stoa also separated the Temple and the Antonia. The term "in double rows" means that there was a series of columns 15 cubits away from the wall and another series 30 cubits away. The Talmud (Pesachim 12b) makes reference to the double stoa.

"Passing across the courtyard toward the second court of the Temple, one found it surrounded by a stone fence, 3 cubits high, a very fine piece of work. Upon it, at intervals, stood stone slabs giving warning, some in Greek, others in Latin, of the law of sanctity and that non-Jews were prohibited from entering the holy area."

Most commentaries assumed that the fence, the Soreg, was made of wooden slats 10 fists (t'fachim) high. Josephus tells us that it was made of stone and was 3 cubits (18 fists) high. One commentary mentioned earlier (Tavnis Haichel) said the wooden fence was built atop a stone fence 1 cubit high. One cubit plus 10 t'fachim is about 3 cubits. Earlier we mentioned that two of the stones' engravings, carved in Greek, have been discovered.

"The second courtyard was approached by fourteen steps, for it was elevated upon a quadrangle." (The Mishna says twelve steps.) "It had walls of its own, on the outside 40 cubits in height, but this was partially hidden by the steps. From the inside of the elevated second platform, the wall rose upward 25 cubits. Beyond the fourteen steps there was a level terrace of 10 cubits between the top of the steps and the wall. From this terrace other flights of steps, five steps each, led up to the gates."

The walls of the second courtyard were retaining walls 40 cubits high. The lower portion of the wall was not visible because the steps that surrounded the wall blocked it from view. Since the retaining wall was 40 cubits high and only 25 cubits of height could be seen within the courtyard, the courtyard must have been 15 cubits higher than the lower courtyard. The Mishna tells us that the Women's Courtyard was 6 cubits higher than the outer floor level. This is a discrepancy of 9 cubits. Also, the Mishna states that each Temple step was half a cubit high. According to Josephus's description 15 cubits would have required thirty steps, not the fourteen he reported.

An approach to reconciling this discrepancy could be as follows. The Mishna is describing an eastern approach to the Women's Courtyard. As that courtyard was 6 cubits higher than the outer floor, it would require twelve steps. Josephus is describing a northern or southern approach to the Azarah. The Azarah was 10 cubits higher than the Women's Courtyard to the east. An additional twenty steps would be needed along the northern and southern walls. Josephus is describing these additional twenty steps. There were fourteen steps; atop the fourteenth step was a landing 10 cubits wide; at the end of the landing were another five steps that led into the northern or southern side of the Azarah. We determined that twenty steps would be needed, Josephus only gave us nineteen. Perhaps the landing sloped upward half a cubit, taking the place of the missing step. From Josephus we determined that the Azarah was 15 cubits higher than the outer floor level. The Mishna tells us it was 16 cubits higher. Although there is one opinion that says the Azarah was only 15 cubits higher (Midos 2:6), since the halachic consensus is not in agreement with that opinion, it is more likely that Josephus was not totally accurate in his estimation of the heights, and that he erred by one cubit.

"There were eight gates, four on the north and four on the south. There were two on the east. They were necessary, for in that eastern quarter a special place was walled off for the women, thus requiring a second gate which faced the first. On the other sides of the Women's Courtyard there was one gate to the north and one gate to the south. The women did not enter the other gates, nor pass by the partition wall of their own gate. There western wall of the second courtyard had no gate."

In *Antiquities*, Josephus says there were three gates to the north and three to the south. Perhaps here (*The Jewish War*) he is counting the north and south gates of the Women's Courtyard and in

Antiquities he was not; or perhaps here (*The Jewish War*) he is counting all the gates of the northern and southern side, large and small, and in *Antiquities* he was only counting the large gateways. One gate on the southern side, the Upper Gate, was a small gateway, and one gateway on the northern side, the Women's Gate was small.

Josephus says there was no western gate. The Mishna states that there were two. Earlier we reconciled that contradiction. Before Herod there were two gates, but during the Herodian reconstruction, the foundations in the western sector fell and the gates were never completed.

"Stoas were between the gates inside the walls facing the chambers. They rested on beautiful high columns. These stoas were a single row of columns, and other than size were in no way inferior to the stoas of the lower court." (In *Antiquities*, on the other hand, Josephus says that the eastern wall had a double stoa.)

"Nine of the gates were completely overlaid with gold and silver, as were the lintels and doorposts. The one gate outside the Sanctuary was of Corinthian bronze and excelled those of gold and silver." (**Note**: Josephus here [*The Jewish War*] refers to the Nicanor Gate. The nine plated gateways were four on the northern side of the Azarah, four on the southern side, and the entrance to the Heichel.) "Each gateway had two doors. Each door was 30 cubits high and 15 cubits wide." (**Note**: In many instances Josephus gives us an incorrect number of cubits. Often he overestimates by one and a half. Here the numbers should be 20 and 10. Possibly Josephus is referring to some other cubit than the halachic measure.) "Inside the gateways, away from the opening, on either side were gaterooms measuring 30 cubits in length and width. They were shaped like towers over 40 cubits high, each room supported by two columns 12 cubits in circumference. All the gates were the same size, except the one opposite the Corinthian gate on the eastern side of the holy House. It was 50 cubits high with doors 40 cubits."

Josephus here refers to the entrance into the hall or portico before the Heichel, which was opposite the Corinthian or Nicanor Gate. It was 40 cubits high and above the entranceway were five rows of wood beams projecting from the wall, separated by rows of projecting stones. Each row was 1 cubit high. If these decorative beams and stones are counted as part of the entranceway, the height would be 50 cubits. However, the use of the word "doors" is peculiar because that gateway had no doors, only curtains. Perhaps it is a poor translation from the original Greek.

"Its decoration was more magnificent, the gold and silver plates being much thicker. This plating was the gift of Alexander, the father of Tiberius."

Here, I assume, Josephus is describing the doors of the Heichel (Kodesh), not the entranceway to the hall or portico, which had no doors. Or perhaps the walls of the entranceway were gold-plated. Alexander was famed for his piety and generosity. His son, Tiberius, a renegade Jew, was one of Titus's chiefs of staff, and helped destroy Jerusalem.

"Fifteen steps led up from the women's enclosure to the great gate [Nicanor Gate]. These steps were five less than the steps that led up to the other gates."

As explained earlier, along the northern and southern sides of the Azarah were twenty steps (nineteen steps plus the landing), as well as the twelve steps that led up to the level of the Women's Courtyard. Here Josephus says that fifteen steps led up from the Women's Courtyard to the Nicanor Gate. These are five fewer steps than the twenty.

"The Sanctuary itself stood in the center and was reached by a flight of twelve steps. Its facade was 100 cubits high and 100 cubits wide. The rear of the building was only 60 cubits wide for the front extended 20 cubits in either direction."

The "20 cubits" is an overestimation of one and a half. The figure should be 15 cubits, which changes the rear of the Heichel from 60 cubits to 70 cubits.

"The first gate was 70 cubits high and 25 cubits broad." (**Note**: Should read 40 cubits high and 20 cubits broad.) "It had no doors for it represented the heavens." (Because the doors of Heaven are never shut.) "The entire surface was covered with gold." (The inner walls were plated with gold.) "Through the doorway the entire Kodesh was visible, towering upward 90 cubits." (The total height was 100 cubits. Excluding the six-cubit foundation and four-cubit wall around the roof, the height of the building was 90 cubits.) "It was 50 [61] cubits long and 20 cubits wide. The Kodesh was two stories high and appeared lower from within than from without. Its golden doors were 55 [20] cubits high and 16 [10] cubits broad. The gateway opening into the building was, as I said, overlaid with gold as were the walls within surrounding it. Above the doorway hung the golden grapevine, from which hung grape clusters as tall as a man. In front of this was a curtain of equal length of the gateway. It was a Babylonian tapestry embroidered with blue, scarlet, purple, and fine linen done with marvelous craftsmanship. The materials had mystical significance; they represented the universe. The scarlet denoted fire, for fire is red. The fine linen denoted the earth, for linen comes from the earth. Blue represented the heavens, for the sky is blue. Purple denoted the sea, for the purple dye came from the sea. Worked into the curtain were the mysteries of the heavens, except the twelve signs of the Zodiac which were not depicted.

"Passing within, one entered the Sanctuary. It was 60 [40] cubits in height and [61 cubits in] length, its width was 20 cubits. Its length was divided, the first 40 cubits contained three of the most wonderful things, the Menorah, the Table, and an Altar. The innermost chamber measured 20 cubits, and was separated from the outer section by a curtain. Nothing stood in it. It was unapproachable to all. Around the sides of the lower part of the Sanctuary were many intercommunicating rooms, three stories high. They could be approached by passages from either side of the gateway. [Although the southern passageway was never used.] The upper story had no chambers around it and so was narrower than the lower portion. The upper portion was 40 cubits [49 including the ceiling and wall around the roof]. Together with the lower 60 cubits [51 cubits, including the foundation and ceiling of the Kodesh], the total height is 100 cubits.

"Overlaid on all sides of the exterior were plates of gold which reflected the sun's first rays. [Should read, "Overlaid outside the door was a plate of gold. . . ."] It shone so brightly that it forced one to look away. The Sanctuary looked like a snow-clad mountain rising upward. From the top rose sharp spikes to prevent birds from perching on top. Some of the stones in the building were 45 cubits in length, 5 cubits in height, and 6 deep." (In *Yosiphon* and in *Antiquities* the numbers are 25, 8, and 12.) "Before the Sanctuary stood the Altar, 15 [10] cubits high and 50 [32] cubits in length and width with the four corners protruding upward. It was approached from the south by a ramp. It was built without metal and no metal ever touched it. A low stone wall, 1 cubit high, partitioned off the Altar and the Sanctuary which was the domain of the priests." (The 1-cubit partition may refer to the bottom "step" going up from the Courtyard of the Israelites into the Courtyard of the Priests, which was 1-cubit high—the only 1-cubit step in the Temple.)

Other than the numbers Josephus gives us, his description is no different from that of the Talmud and Mishna. Do we have any evidence that Josephus ever set foot in the Temple? During the final years of the Second Temple, the Zealots were in control of the Temple, and Josephus was their sworn enemy. Is it possible, then, that Josephus had no firsthand knowledge of the Temple?

In his autobiography, Josephus does say that he spent some time in the Temple. He had just completed a trip to Rome to help obtain the release of several priests who were cast into bondage. Josephus did not wish to appear to be a Roman sympathizer, so upon returning from Rome, he spent some time in the Temple Compound. He had left for Rome at age 26, in 63 C.E. How long the journey took and how long he remained in Rome is not known. From his accounts of various adventures and misadventures, it was not a short trip. It would seem that the journey to Rome took at least one year, probably more. Josephus departed from the Temple when the Zealot Menachem was captured and killed. This happened on the Tenth of Elul in 66 C.E. Thus Josephus spent anywhere from a month to two years in the Temple.

APPENDIX

The Third Temple

This is the commentary of Rabbi Tosfos Yom Tov Heller on the portion of the book of Ezekiel that deals with the prophetic Third Temple (see Plate 104). It is called Tzuras HaBayis. I have included, parenthetically, other commentaries (Malbim and Vilna Gaon) that clarify or disagree as the case may be.

"A wall surrounds the Temple Mount [Plate 113] along the eastern, northern, western, and southern sides. The length of each wall is 500 measures. Each measure is 6 cubits. Each cubit is 6 fists, t'fachim. Therefore, the length of each wall is 3,000 cubits, each cubit being 6 fists. The thickness of each wall is 1 measure. The height of the eastern wall is 1 measure as explained in verse 5 of chapter 40. However, the height of the northern, western, and southern walls is not mentioned in the text.

"Another wall surrounds a courtyard, known as the Women's Courtyard. Its inside expanse from east to west is 317 cubits [326 (Malbim)] and the inside expanse from north to south is 312 cubits [326 (Malbim)]. The thickness of the wall was 1 measure [13 cubits (Malbim)].

"In the middle of the eastern wall is a gateway 10 cubits wide and 50 cubits high [measurement of height unknown (Malbim)]. The thickness of the gateway being the same as the thickness of the wall. [Toward the outside of the doorway were two doorposts, each 6 cubits wide. Toward the far side of the doorway were another two doorposts, each also 6 cubits wide. A space of 1 cubit

Plate 113. Byzantine ruins at the southwestern corner of the Temple Mount. The Byzantines, under Constantine the Great, controlled Jerusalem from the early part of the fourth century c.e. Their ruthless rule lasted 300 years.

separated each pair of doorposts. It was there the doors were attached (Malbim)]. From the right of the gateway to the northern wall was 151 cubits [158 (Malbim)], and likewise from the left of the gateway to the southern wall is 151 cubits [158 (Malbim)]. The total length of the eastern wall including the gateway was 312 cubits [(326 (Malbim)], the width of the Women's Courtyard. In the northern and southern walls the gateways were not exactly in the center of the wall [were exactly in the center of the wall (Malbim)]. From the eastern wall to either of those gateways is 141 cubits [158 (Malbim)] but from the western wall to either of those two gateways is 146 cubits [158 (Malbim)]. The total lengths of the northern and southern walls, including the gateway, were 317 cubits [326 (Malbim)], the length of the Women's Courtyard.

"In front of the eastern gateway were twelve steps [(seven steps (Malbim)], for the mountain slopes upward from the base of the Cheil until its top, equal to the height of the twelve steps [seven steps (Malbim)]. In front of the northern and southern gateways were only seven steps, for the mountain sloped higher in the east. [Flanking the base of the steps are stone columns 1 cubit by 1 cubit (Malbim).] The steps were flanked by small offices. [Between the steps is a platform. In front of the platform are the steps (Malbim).]

"Outside each gateway, to the right and left, are small chambers. [The chambers were inside the courtyard (Vilna Gaon).] There are three to the left of the gateway and three to the right of the gateway. [The eastern chambers did not go from north to south, but rather from east to west. Likewise, the northern and southern chambers did not go from east to west, but rather from north to south (Vilna Gaon).] The inside length of each chamber is 1 measure, and the inside width of each chamber is 1 measure. The walls outside each chamber and the walls between each chamber are 5 cubits. [There were no adjoining walls between chambers, rather there was a gap of 5 cubits space (Vilna Gaon).] [The wall of a chamber nearest to the gateway is 6 cubits thick; likewise the wall of a chamber farthest from a gateway was 6 cubits (Malbim).] The wall of the Women's Courtyard served as the back wall of the chambers. [Even the chambers that were next to the wall of the courtyard had their own wall of 1 cubit in thickness (Vilna Gaon).] The space between the three chambers to the right of the doorway and the left of the doorway is 15 cubits, 10 cubits being the steps leading up into the courtyard and each set of chambers were set away from the steps 2½ cubits. [The space between the three chambers to the left of the gateway and the three chambers to the right of the gateway is 10 cubits, the width of the doorway (Malbim).]

"Each set of three chambers has doors leading from the first chamber into the second and from the second into the third. There are no doors on the outside wall of the chambers. Flanking each door are tall narrow windows. [Also flanking each door leading to the gateway, were stone columns, 1 cubit by 1 cubit (Malbim)]. There are also windows set into the back wall of each chamber. The chambers by the eastern gate have windows in the front wall of each chamber.

"Inside each gateway is a portico consisting of two parallel walls leading from the gateway inward 8 cubits [6 cubits (Malbim)]. The thickness of each wall is 6 cubits and the height is 50 cubits [measurement of the height is not known (Malbim)], the same as the height of the gateway. The width of the portico is 13 cubits, the width of the gateway being 10 cubits and each wall set back 1½ cubits from the gateway [width of the portico is 10 cubits, the same as the gateway (Malbim)]. Tall narrow windows are set into the walls of the portico.

"At the end of the walls of the portico, set against the thickness of the wall, are two elliptical columns. The columns completely cover the thickness of the wall, which are 6 cubits thick. The columns extend outward 2 cubits. The height of the columns is 60 cubits. Therefore, the total length of the portico is 10 cubits including the columns. [Along the inside of the wall at each end, are stone columns, 1 cubit by 1 cubit. This so by all the walls of all the porticos (Malbim).]

"Above each column is a capital shaped like a date tree. [The capital consisted of two date trees opposite each other (Vilna Gaon).]

"In the four corners of the Women's Courtyard is a large roofless chamber [40 cubits from east to west, and 30 cubits from north to south (Malbim)]. A colonnade goes from each gateway until each roofless chamber. A colonnade is a series of columns supporting a roof. Built atop the roof were chambers, thirty in all, going around the four sides of the Women's Courtyard. [The chambers are built on ground level. They are only along the northern, eastern, and southern walls. Five chambers are to the left of each gateway and five chambers are to the right of each gateway (Malbim).] [These chambers were three stories high. The bottom story was the largest. The top story was the smallest (Vilna Gaon).]

"A wall surrounds an inner courtyard called the Courtyard of the

Israelites. The length of the inside expanse from east to west is 100 cubits. The width from north to south is 100 cubits. The distance between the southern wall of the Courtyard of the Israelites and the southern wall of the Women's Courtyard is 100 cubits. Likewise, the distance between the northern walls is 100 cubits. In the middle of each wall is a gateway 10 cubits wide and 50 cubits high [height unknown (Malbim)], opposite each gateway of the Women's Courtyard. Therefore, from the right side of each gateway to the next adjacent wall is 45 cubits, and from the left side of each gateway to the next adjacent wall is 45 cubits. There is no wall on the western side of the Courtyard of the Israelites, for the Hall of the Heichel is there. [There was a wall along the western side of the Courtyard of the Israelites, 3 cubits thick (Vilna Gaon).] The thickness of each wall is 6 cubits [13 cubits (Malbim)].

"Just as the gateways of the Women's Courtyard have small chambers and porticos, so do the gateways of the Courtyard of the Israelites, except the porticos of the Courtyard of the Israelites are outside the gateway and the porticos of the Women's Courtyard are inside the gateways. In this way the porticos face each other and are most beautiful. The porticos outside the Courtyard of the Israelites start from the outside walls of the chambers and not from the wall of the courtyard itself.

"Eight steps lead from the Women's Courtyard into the Courtyard of the Israelites through each of the three gateways. [Flanking the base of the steps were stone columns, 1 cubit by 1 cubit, with capitals in the form of date trees (Malbim).]

"Inside the portico of the northern gateway of the Courtyard of the Israelites are four tables. Two tables are to the east and two tables are to the west. Although this portico is actually located within the Women's Courtyard, its sanctity is that of the Courtyard of the Israelites [the sanctity extended to 2 cubits beyond the portico (Malbim)]. In the area between the three offices to the west and the three offices to the east of that gateway, are also four tables. Two are to the west and two are to the east. [Each set of tables flanked the doorway of the chamber. Eight more tables were located within the northern gateway itself. All these tables were for slaughtering the Holiest sacrifices—kodshai kodashim (Malbim).]

"A chamber is built in the Courtyard of the Israelites which opens into the northern gateway. It is called the Chamber of the Slaughtering Area. [No chamber was built there. It was merely a designated area called the slaughtering area (Malbim).] In it are four stone tables. The length of each table is 1½ cubits, the width of each table is 1½ cubits, and the height of each table is 1 cubit. Upon them are placed knives and bowls, prepared for those who are to slaughter the burnt offerings. Along the four walls of the chamber are small columns with pegs or hooks projecting outward 1 cubit. Upon these hooks the offerings are hung and flayed. [The columns and hooks were located to the west of the northern gate (Malbim).] [The hooks were set into the walls of the small chambers flanking the gateway (Vilna Gaon).]

"Two chambers are built near the northern gateway toward the east. These are for the Levites who serve as watchmen and guards. [These chambers were for the priests who were unfit to serve. They would assist the Levites (Malbim). Unfit due to their previous idolatry (Vilna Gaon).] The doors to these chambers are on the southern side of these rooms. Another chamber is located against this wall near the eastern wall. It is for the priests who watch the service of the Altar. [This chamber was built against the southern wall near the ramp of the Altar, toward the east (Malbim).] Its door is on the northern side.

"The Altar stands in the Courtyard of the Israelites. It is 34 cubits from the eastern wall and 34 cubits from the front of the Hall before the Heichel. The center of the Altar is opposite the center of the Heichel. The 34 cubits between the Altar and the eastern wall is divided into two sections. The first 17 cubits is for the Israelites and the second 17 cubits is for the priests.

"Built inside the wall are hallways. [These hallways were built inside the courtyard along the wall. The hallways began 15 cubits away from each gateway (Malbim).] One to the left of each gateway, and one to the right. The length of each hallway is 25 cubits and the width is 5 cubits."

C APPENDIX

The Temple Scroll

During the Six Day War, amid the shelling and bombing, cloaked in mystery and intrigue, the Israeli government procured an ancient scroll. It was one of the Dead Sea Scrolls and dealt in great part with the Jewish Temple. It has been called The Temple Scroll.

The scroll describes the Temple as consisting of three concentric square courtyards. The innermost yard was either 280 cubits by 280 cubits or 140 cubits by 140 cubits. Much of the scroll has been damaged or is missing so the correct dimensions cannot be ascertained. Exactly what this courtyard was we do not know. Neither number, 140 or 280, had come up before. Perhaps the author of the scroll pictured the Women's Courtyard forming a rectangle around the sacred precinct of the Azarah, with its Altar and Heichel. The width of the Women's Courtyard all around the Azarah would have been 135 cubits. That does not include the thickness of the Women's Courtyard's wall. If it was 5 cubits, that would give us the necessary 140 cubits. However, I should hasten to point out that all the rabbinic commentators maintain that the Women's Courtyard did not surround the Azarah but rather was located to the east of the Azarah.

In one of the Dead Sea Caves, a cloth was found on which were depicted four concentric rectangles. Perhaps it was a representation of the Temple. The fourth square represents either the Herodian extension or the city of Jerusalem. The scroll mentions an entranceway in each wall of this inner 140/280 cubit courtyard. The

Women's Courtyard did in fact have an entranceway in each of its four walls.

Only a few words about the Altar are left preserved. ". . . all built of stones . . . 20 . . . to corner. . . ." The text probably read ". . . all built of stones, 20 cubits from corner to corner." The question now arises, where do we find any dimension of the Altar given as 20 cubits? In the Second Temple and in Ezekiel's vision we do not find reference to these 20 cubits. However, in the First Temple the Altar was in fact 20 cubits by 20 cubits on its top surface. The Altar was smaller than the Second Temple Altar (2 Chronicles 4:1; Midos 3:1). Is it possible that this scroll is describing the First Temple and not the Second?

The Temple Scroll relates that the middle courtyard surrounded the inner yard, and a space of 100 cubits separated them. Instead of trying to reconcile this with existing rabbinic literature, let us proceed to the Temple Scroll's depiction of the outer courtyard. The scroll says, "And you shall make an outer yard around the middle court about one thousand six hundred cubits from edge to edge." This 1,600 cubits presents a real problem. The First and Second Temples were only 500 cubits. Even including the Herodian extension of the Second Temple, it was only about 1,100 cubits long. Ezekiel's Third Temple was to have an outer wall of 3,000 cubits. There is no reasonable way that this figure of 1,600 cubits can be reconciled historically or halachically.

There are a multitude of other problems that the scroll presents from a historical and halachic perspective. It more properly requires a treatise of its own. However, based on what we have presented here, the scroll was obviously not a historical account of the First or Second Temples; it was a rival or competing text to the Book of Ezekiel. When the Sages of the Great Assembly convened in the third century B.C.E. to decide which religious texts should be included in the Sacred Scriptures, the Temple Scroll was obviously not one of them. Why then would the Essenes of Qumran continue to copy and hold onto this scripture?

It appears to me that Essenes were a renegade cult. They had their own collection of sacred scriptures. They had their own calendar. They lived a monklike existence. From Josephus's description of this cult, images of monastaries and friars come to mind. Perhaps the Essenes were the forerunners of Christianity. When the Christian movement began, perhaps the two groups synthesized and merged.

What the relationship between these Essenes and the rabbinic

Pharisees was we do not know. The Essenes did live in ancient Jerusalem; one of the city gates was called the Essene Gate. Did they worship in the Temple? Did they accept the Second Temple as holy? Did the Temple priests accept them as worthy participants? Did any of the actual observations of the Essenes find their way into their scrolls? As I mentioned earlier, the Temple Scroll and its authors require a treatise of their own.

Temple Chronology

830	B.C.E.	Solomon begins building First Temple
823	B.C.E.	Solomon completes First Temple
420	B.C.E.	First Temple destroyed by Babylonian Emperor Nebuchadnezzar. Jews exiled
368	B.C.E.	Persian Emperor Cyrus grants Jews permission to rebuild Temple
366	B.C.E.	Persian Emperor Artaxerxes halts construction
350	B.C.E.	Persian Emperor Darius gives Jews permission to continue building Second Temple
346	B.C.E.	Second Temple completed
310	B.C.E.	Simon the Just makes treaty with Alexander the Great
142	B.C.E.	Greek-Syrian Emperor Antiochus captures Temple, begins pagan worship in the Temple
136	B.C.E.	Judah Maccabee regains Temple. Miracle of the Menorah
63	B.C.E.	Roman Emperor Pompey conquers Judea
16	B.C.E.	Herod extends and rebuilds Second Temple
70	C.E.	Roman General Titus destroys Second Temple
135	C.E.	Roman Emperor Hadrian puts down Bar Kokhba revolt, builds pagan temple atop the Temple Mount
326	C.E.	Byzantine era, Emperor Constantine

363	C.E.	Julian the Apostate gives Jews permission to rebuild Temple. Julian dies one year later
364	C.E.	Jovian prohibits Jews in Jerusalem
614	C.E.	Persians conquer Jerusalem. Jews given permission to rebuild Temple. Christians riot. Permission withdrawn
629	C.E.	Byzantine Heraculius recaptures Jerusalem
637	C.E.	Muslims conquer Holy Land
690	C.E.	Muslim construction of the Dome of the Rock begins
715	C.E.	El Aksa completed
868	C.E.	Holy Land annexed to Egypt
1099	C.E.	Christian Crusaders capture Jerusalem
1187	C.E.	Saladin recaptures Jerusalem for Muslims
1229	C.E.	Jerusalem yielded to Holy Roman Emperor and King of Germany Frederick II
1244	C.E.	Jerusalem under Turkish Tartars
1260	C.E.	Jerusalem under the Mongols
1267	C.E.	Jerusalem under Egyptian Mamelukes
1517	C.E.	Ottoman Rule
1917	C.E.	British capture Palestine
1948	C.E.	Establishment of the State of Israel. Jerusalem divided
1967	C.E.	Jerusalem united

Keys to Plate 76

Alphabetical

Altar–40
Atvinus Chamber–24
Chamber of Oils–9
Chamber of Pinchus the
     Clothier–14
Chamber of the High Priest–19
Chamber of the High Priest's
     Meal Offering–15
Chamber of the Instruments–11
Chamber of the Lepers–8
Chamber of the Nazirites–6
Chamber of the Receipts–36
Chamber of the Showbread–35
Chamber of the Well–20
Chamber of the Wood–7
Chambers of the Knives–46
Cheil–2
cistern (water downpour area)–53
Courtyard of the Priests–17
columns (Butchering Place)–37
court, lower judicial–5
duchan (Courtyard of the
     Israelites)–16
fence (Soreg)–1
Gate of Sparks–29

Gate of the Firewood–26
Gate of the Firstborn Offering–25
Hall (Heichel)–45
Hall entrance (Heichel)–44
Hearth–32
Hearth Chamber–34
Heichel–47
Heichel, outer wall with
     windows–52
Holy of Holies–48
hooks (Butchering Place)–37
hoops (Butchering Place)–39
Kodesh–47
Kodesh HaKadashim–48
Lower Gate–3
mikva (Water Gate)–24
mikva entrance (Hearth
     Chamber)–34
Nicanor Gate–12
Palhedron Chamber–19
Parvah Chamber–22
platform (Courtyard of the
     Israelites)–16
ramp–15
Rinser's Chamber–30

Hebrew

BIBLIOGRAPHY

Avi-Yonah, M. (1972). *The Holy Land*. New York: Holt, Rinehart.

Avigad, N. (1983). *Discovering Jerusalem*. Jerusalem: Shokmona Publishing Company.

Ben-Arieh, Y. (1979). *The Rediscovery of the Holy Land in the Nineteenth Century*. Detroit: Wayne State University Press.

Ben-Dov, M. (1982). *In the Shadow of the Temple*. NewYork: Harper and Row.

Ben-Dov, M., Naor, M., and Aner, Z. (1983). *The Western Wall*. Jerusalem: Ministry of Defense.

Bishko, H. (1983). *This Is Jerusalem*. Tel Aviv: Heritage Publishing.

Cornfeld, G. (1982). *Josephus, The Jewish War*. Grand Rapids, MI: Zondervan.

Eisenstein, J. D. (1952). *Otzar Yisroel*. New York: Pardes.

Hominer, H. (1971). *Josiphon*. Jerusalem: Hominer.

Jerusalem (1973). Jerusalem: Keter.

Josephus, Flavius (1957). *Jewish Antiquities*. Trans. William Whiston. Philadelphia: John C. Winston Co.

Kenyon, K. M. (1967). *Jerusalem: Excavating 3,000 Years of History*. New York: McGraw Hill.

———— (1974). *Digging Up Jerusalem*. New York: Praeger.

Mare, W. H. (1987). *The Archaeology of the Jerusalem Area*. Grand Rapids, MI: Baker Book House.

Mazar, B. (1975). *The Mountain of the Lord*. Garden City, NY: Doubleday.

Sharon, A. (1973). *Planning Jerusalem*. New York: McGraw Hill.

Schiller, E. (1978). *The El Aksa Mosque*. Jerusalem: Ariel.

Vilnay, Z. (1978). *Legends of Jerusalem*. Philadelphia: The Jewish Publication Society.

Wilson, Capt. C. W. (1980). *Ordnance Survey of Jerusalem 1866*. Facsimile edition. Jerusalem: Ariel.

————(1980). *Jerusalem, the Holy City*. Jerusalem: Ariel.

Yadin, Y. (1975). *Jerusalem Revealed*. Jerusalem: The Israel Exploration Society.

———— (1978). *Bar Kokhba*. London: Weidenfeld & Nicolson.

———— (1985). *The Temple Scroll*. New York: Random House.